MYTHS & LEGENDS OF MASTERY

IN THE
MATHEMATICS CURRICULUM

Sara Miller McCune founded SAGE Publishing in 1965 to support the dissemination of usable knowledge and educate a global community. SAGE publishes more than 1000 journals and over 800 new books each year, spanning a wide range of subject areas. Our growing selection of library products includes archives, data, case studies and video. SAGE remains majority owned by our founder and after her lifetime will become owned by a charitable trust that secures the company's continued independence.

Los Angeles | London | New Delhi | Singapore | Washington DC | Melbourne

MYTHS & LEGENDS OF MASTERY

IN THE MATHEMATICS CURRICULUM

PINKY JAIN
ROSALYN HYDE

LM Learning Matters

Learning Matters
A SAGE Publishing Company
1 Oliver's Yard
55 City Road
London EC1Y 1SP

SAGE Publications Inc.
2455 Teller Road
Thousand Oaks, California 91320

SAGE Publications India Pvt Ltd
B 1/I 1 Mohan Cooperative Industrial Area
Mathura Road
New Delhi 110 044

SAGE Publications Asia-Pacific Pte Ltd
3 Church Street
#10-04 Samsung Hub
Singapore 049483

Editor: Amy Thornton
Senior project editor: Chris Marke
Project management: Swales & Willis Ltd, Exeter, Devon
Marketing manager: Lorna Patkai
Cover design: Wendy Scott
Typeset by: C&M Digitals (P) Ltd, Chennai, India
Printed in the UK

Library of Congress Control Number: 2020932148

British Library Cataloguing in Publication data

A catalogue record for this book is available from the British Library

ISBN 978-1-5264-4678-7
ISBN 978-1-5264-4679-4 (pbk)

CONTENTS

ABOUT THE EDITORS AND CONTRIBUTORS

The editors

Pinky Jain is Principal Lecturer in Primary Education at the University of Worcester. She leads on international development and primary mathematics. Pinky is passionate about education, especially the professional development of student teachers and the teaching of mathematics in schools. Her research interests include the development of mathematical reasoning and the use of narrative and talk in enhancing conceptual understanding of mathematics.

Rosalyn Hyde is Principal Teaching Fellow in Mathematics Education at the University of Southampton and teaches on PGCE and master's programmes. Her research interests include mathematics pedagogy and mastery approaches at Key Stage 3, initial teacher education, and teaching mathematics with digital technology.

The contributors

Rosa Archer is Senior Lecturer in Mathematics Education at the University of Manchester, where she leads the secondary PGCE mathematics team. She is passionate about mathematics and about teaching. All of her research is aimed at making the learning experience a good one for young people as well as teachers. Her particular interests are in lesson study and in subject knowledge for teachers. She is currently working on using lesson study to provide professional development for experienced teachers alongside student teachers.

Sally Bamber is Senior Lecturer in Mathematics Education at the University of Chester. Her research interests are in collaborative mathematics classroom enquiry; developing pedagogy to increase the accessibility and enjoyment of mathematics education for 8–18-year-olds. She is interested in developing transformative teacher education models that merge continuous and initial teacher education with research-informed classroom enquiry.

Diane Cochrane is Senior Lecturer in Mathematics Education at the University of Wolverhampton across primary and secondary initial teacher education programmes. She was previously a mathematics teacher and has prior experience working as an advanced skills teacher and as a consultant, supporting colleagues in a variety of schools and delivering professional development.

Helen Farmery is Senior Lecturer in Primary Mathematics at Middlesex University in London and has several years of experience teaching in primary schools in North London. She works closely with her student teachers and the schools they are placed in to develop innovative and creative classroom teachers. Her research interest is in cultural responsivity in mathematics, and her action research has been in the development of the Numicon approach and in her work with children experiencing mathematical difficulties as part of the Every Child Counts programme.

Louise Hoskyns-Staples is an independent mathematics teacher educator. Her research interests include the teacher pedagogy in textbooks written for a mastery curriculum and summative assessment. She has a breadth of experience in mathematics education, having worked as the mathematics lead in both primary and secondary schools and as a primary head teacher.

Anne Mulligan is Senior Lecturer at Middlesex University in London, where she teaches primary mathematics on the initial teacher education programmes. She has over 20 years of experience teaching in the primary classroom, specialising in Key Stage 1, and spent four years as a deputy head teacher before moving to teacher education. Whilst a deputy head teacher she completed her doctoral study through action research into the impact of changes in classroom practice on children's ability to problem-solve.

Mary O'Connor is a Lecturer in Mathematics Education at the University of Birmingham. She currently leads the secondary PGCE courses at the University of Birmingham Dubai where she also teaches the PGCE mathematics course. At the home campus in Birmingham, Mary teaches on both the mathematics PGDipEd and the mathematics Subject Knowledge Enhancement Course. Mary is an active member of the AMET Committee and holds the post of Treasurer of AMET. Prior to working in higher education, Mary taught mathematics for many years at schools in the West Midlands and the Middle East and has a wealth of experience as a Lead mathematics teacher, head of department, and a head of sixth form.

Tom Weaver is Senior Lecturer at the University of Worcester, where he lectures in primary initial teacher education and more widely on the children and families sector. Tom's research centres on the subtleties of teacher–learner interaction and the practical implications of teaching and activity theory.

INTRODUCTION

Mastery – this is a loaded word that provokes a plethora of responses within mathematics educators and teachers alike. Whether we personally agree or disagree with the use of the term or concept, which has been promoted by the global ranking and comparison agenda, there is much needed debate. Currently, there is no agreement as to what this term means and, more importantly, how it might be operationalised. Since the introduction of this term, a multitude of approaches have been used in schools implementing what might be called 'mastery' teaching of mathematics. Furthermore, within the mathematics education world, there is some discussion around what is meant by mastery on an implicit level. What this really means in terms of our teaching and pedagogical structures and thinking within schools is starting to be considered. There is much confusion in both the primary and secondary worlds around the practical implications of mastery and its many interpretations. The conflicting worlds of Ofsted, good pedagogical choices, needs of learners, tracking of progress, and our own values regarding teaching and learning have all come to the fore when considering and defining mastery. The challenge from the East has also raised philosophical questions about our own educational principles and social beliefs about learning mathematics.

All this messy confusion continues to be quite positive, on the one hand, as it means we are looking at what our personal and system positions might be in ensuring that we have a developed approach to mathematics education. On the other hand, the lack of agreement does make it challenging to lead on decisions within schools in ensuring that all are interpreting this notion of mastery in a consistent manner. The challenge for schools is in choosing the right ways forward when there are so many other conflicting agendas. Furthermore, the range of interpretations means that there are no cohesive practices across all schools. What is needed is support for teachers, mathematics leads and schools in the formulation of a contextualised interpretation of mastery and guidance as to how to move forward within not just local settings, but also in the wider system. If indeed there is a very local approach needed to ensure that we are teaching for mastery (however it is defined), the question might be: Why write this book?

Our aim is to allow you to put a comma in your time and help you to unpick the choices you are making using an evidence-based approach in order to develop your own definition of teaching for mastery and your own understanding of the consequent implications on your practice. We believe that one overarching definition is not the way forward. What is needed is to define the principles that make up mastery and how you might operationalise these. This is therefore an area that needs development, clarification and deeper understanding (we might say mastery) of what is meant by this complex and overused term. Mastery is the ultimate aim of any learning goal. We learn to develop skills and a depth in our ability to make knowledge in order to move from functional to creative and to be able to apply this understanding to make new knowledge, be it our own or new to all. Therefore, this book will unpick the notion of mastery with a specific focus on mathematics to develop a clear understanding of how we can apply this to our teaching. In terms of mastery, there are a range of matters that need to be explained and explored, and at this stage it is important to make our stand clear. Mastery, in our view, is not new in its current definition as a South East Asian import, and therefore the overuse, or misuse, of this term is a key motivation driving us to write this book. We believe that mastery (deep conceptual understanding) is the ultimate goal of any learning, and hence the key questions that will be addressed in this book are:

1. What does it mean to 'master' mathematics?

2. How do learners master mathematics?

3. Can learners of all ages master mathematics?

4. Is mastery something that can be taught or ever achieved?

5. What factors affect the effective implementation of mastery approaches within our education system?

This book reflects the journeys of the chapter authors in developing an understanding of current developments under the banner of 'mastery' in mathematics teaching in England. We are not aiming to give you a singular definition of mastery, but to allow you to gain and build tools that will enable you to structure programmes and evaluate what you mean by mastery based on evidence and debate.

This book has been put together by members of the Association of Mathematics Education Teachers (AMET), who are well placed in their experience to consider this complex area from a range of perspectives. AMET is the voice of mathematics teacher educators in the UK, with membership drawn predominantly from the initial teacher education (ITE) community.

For nearly 30 years, the association has been providing a forum for cutting-edge thinking, ideas and practice to be shared and refined by those working with new teachers in both primary and secondary phases. AMET's annual conferences bring a like-minded community together to celebrate, inform and develop mathematics teacher education. The association is always particularly keen to support those new to ITE. AMET is a participating body of the Joint Mathematical Council, an organisation that makes representation and responds to enquiries from government and other policymakers on the advancement of the teaching of mathematics. This is an important forum for the ITE mathematics tutor voice to be heard.

This book has been developed by AMET committee members who are keen to capture the community's current thinking on mastery and establish that the pedagogy underpinning mastery approaches is grounded in theory and action research that has been espoused by those in mathematics teacher education for many years.

The chapters in this book will support you in looking at a range of ideas and in developing your own contextually specific approach to mastery based on principles supported by evidence. Fundamentally, all the chapters support an understanding of mastery approaches as developing deep conceptual learning of mathematics leading to knowledge, skills and understanding with which learners can reason with and use to solve problems. Chapter 1 will help you to work on ideas that will support you in defining mastery from a historical and theoretical perspective.

This chapter also considers what mastery means in schools and how it is used in school contexts, and begins to explore some of the implications for teaching and learning. Chapter 2 starts unpicking the key ideas in teaching for mastery and considers how we can support all learners in their understanding of mathematics. Chapter 3 moves on to the next step, that of the coordination of mathematics in a mastery environment, considering key ideas of progression and consistency. Chapter 4 focuses on the vital area of early years and school readiness, looking at how best to prepare very young learners for later mastery, and considers how early mathematics and developing understanding is similar to language acquisition. Chapter 5 tackles the challenges of subject knowledge and the importance of mathematics subject knowledge in supporting teaching for mastery. It further explores ideas in relation to planning and progression in subject knowledge. Chapter 6 takes a broader perspective, drawing out lessons learnt through the examination of other jurisdictions to identify good practice that can be implemented within the English cultural context. Chapter 7 documents the strengths and shortcomings of two small-scale collaborative mathematics projects to inform the structure of a positive model of teacher education having the potential to transform classrooms. Finally, Chapter 8 considers the real challenge of sustaining mastery and how integration of new staff into school and the philosophy can be supported. It looks at the all-important culture of the school strategies to achieve sufficient mind shift for sustainability of pedagogical approaches.

We hope that the book will not only enable you to consider the complex area of mastery on a personal level, but also support you in the range of roles you may hold, from student teacher or early career teacher to mathematics lead, by providing an evidence-based approach that empowers the pedagogical decision-making process.

Special thanks go to our families and colleagues for their support and long suffering during the writing of this book, and particularly to those hidden individuals who have made this book possible.

1

DEFINING MASTERY

ANNE MULLIGAN AND DIANE COCHRANE

KEYWORDS: MASTERY; DEEP LEARNING; CONCEPTUAL UNDERSTANDING; VARIATION; FLUENCY; REASONING

CHAPTER OBJECTIVES

This chapter will allow you to achieve the following outcomes:

- understand what is meant by 'mastery' in relation to mathematical learning;
- know some of the historical and theoretical background to 'mastery teaching and learning';
- consider some of the implications for schools of developing a mastery approach to teaching and learning mathematics.

Introduction

If we are able to develop mastery learning in students, we must be able to recognize when students have achieved it. We must be able to define what we mean by mastery and we must be able to collect the necessary evidence to establish whether or not a student has achieved it.

(Bloom, 1968, p8)

The term 'mastery' and its use in relation to mathematics teaching and learning in schools is becoming familiar, with teachers adopting a 'mastery approach' and schools using a 'mastery curriculum' and assessing learners as being at 'mastery level'. Before using the term 'mastery' in relation to mathematics, it is important to understand first what is meant by mastery, and second how the term applies to mathematics. It is also worth considering whether schools have a shared understanding of mastery in mathematics and how it is enacted in different school settings.

The National Curriculum makes clear its expectations for all learners by the end of their Key Stage by stating that they will 'know, apply and understand the matters, skills and processes specified in the relevant programme of study' (DfE, 2014, p4), and although it does not explicitly mention mastering the subject, the implication is there. The task for schools then becomes integrating a mastery approach to mathematics with the expectations of the National Curriculum; this, in theory, should be straightforward. The difficulty arises when schools and teachers do not have a clear understanding of what mastery involves and focus more on the term than on its meaning.

It is important to understand why there has come to be such a strong focus on the term 'mastery' in relation to current mathematics teaching. Mastery is not a new idea, but has had a resurgence of interest due to concerns over the performance of English learners in international tests (OECD, 2016; TIMSS, 2015) compared to those in countries such as Singapore and China, who are taught through what we term a 'mastery' approach. Comparisons between the education systems in England and Singapore and Shanghai in China have resulted in some East Asian approaches to teaching being adopted in English schools. Specific aspects include what has become known as 'teaching for mastery' and the use of textbooks. Concrete and manipulative resources are being used more widely as mathematical representations to support learners' conceptual understanding and there is less emphasis on moving through topics quickly.

This chapter aims to define mastery with respect to mathematics teaching and learning. The historical development of mastery from its origins to its current use in schools will be outlined, as well as how it is being interpreted in some settings. Some of the key theoretical perspectives underpinning mastery teaching and learning will be highlighted and some of the implications for schools will be considered.

Defining mastery

What is 'mastery' and what does it mean in terms of mathematics? Various dictionaries define mastery as being comprehensive knowledge or having learnt and understood something to the extent that it can be used without any difficulty. A master is seen as someone who is dominant in a particular field with 'exceptional skills' or knowledge and who is 'thoroughly proficient in their use' (*Collins English Dictionary*, 2006, p528). The implication for mathematics is that learners who have mastered a concept are proficient in the application of the mathematical skills and knowledge associated with that concept. Nunes and Bryant (1998) use the terms 'mastery' or 'mastered' throughout their discussion of children's mathematical understanding. They do not explicitly define the terms, but the implication from their discussion is that when learners have mastered a concept, they are deemed to have a good understanding of that concept, can make connections between it and other concepts, can reason with it, and can apply it in different contexts.

The teaching of mathematics in Shanghai is different to that in England and is considered to take a mastery approach. According to Boylan et al. (2019), it emphasises:

Whole-class interactive teaching to develop conceptual understanding and procedural fluency, using carefully designed tasks and skilful questioning. To ensure pupils progress together, tasks are designed to allow for extension by deepening understanding of concepts and procedures, and daily intervention is used to support those needing extra tuition.

(p15)

Recent approaches to mastery in mathematics are based on East Asian pedagogy, one example being the Mathematics Mastery (2019) programme. This was set up by the Ark network of schools in order to improve attainment of all learners by enabling them to develop deeper conceptual understanding and promote the use of a 'mastery curriculum' based on those of Shanghai and Singapore. It places emphasis on developing depth of understanding rather than breadth of content, and also focuses on whole-class teaching where most learners progress at the same pace. Studying topics in greater depth is intended to reduce the need to revisit topics as often as would normally be the case. The Mathematics Mastery programme also emphasises the importance of language, mathematical representations and having high expectations of learners. The aim of this approach is that learners become fluent in their use of mathematical concepts while developing understanding of them so that deeper conceptual understanding is developed (Vignoles et al., 2015).

While the current National Curriculum does not make specific mention of 'mastery', it is clear that the aims set out in the programmes of study for Key Stages 1–4 require learners to be able to 'become fluent in the fundamentals of mathematics', to 'reason mathematically' and to 'solve problems by applying their mathematics' (DfE, 2014, p4). If learners can successfully achieve these aims, then they would be expected to have mastered the subject to some extent. The importance of developing fluency 'through a deep understanding of mathematical ideas and processes' when attempting to master the subject is noted by Haylock and Cockburn (2017), who also emphasise the need to understand 'mathematical structures' and 'make connections' (p10).

The National Centre for Excellence in the Teaching of Mathematics (NCETM) is a government-funded organisation working to encourage teachers to adopt the ideas of teaching for mastery. It defines mastery in mathematics as a 'deep, long-term, secure and adaptable understanding of the subject', enabling 'pupils to move on to more advanced material' (NCETM, 2016a). In their *Five Big Ideas in Teaching for Mastery* (NCETM, 2019), shown in Figure 1.1, they promote an approach to teaching mathematics based on teaching practices in Shanghai.

Coherence

Coherence is set out as a main component of the teaching for mastery process, enabling learners to realise the potential of connections between mathematical topics previously learnt and working to build on this to develop knowledge. To support this, lessons are planned to contain small episodes of learning, which then connect, leading to generalisations that can be used to support problem-solving in a variety of contexts. This is not a new idea. In fact, it has been fixed at the heart of the National Curriculum since its first version in 1988, where 'Attainment Target 1: Using and Applying Mathematics' contained a variety of ideas within the statements of attainment that described this process. These aimed to lead to learners being able to demonstrate the ability to 'use number, algebra and measures in practical tasks in real-life problems, and to investigate within mathematics itself' (DES and Welsh Office, 1989, p3).

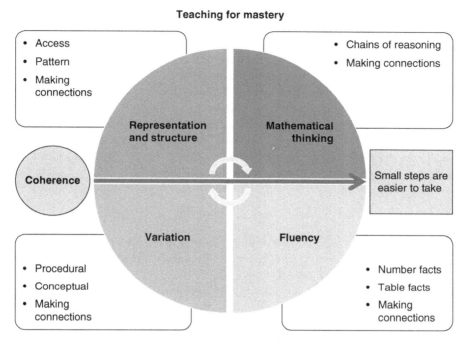

Figure 1.1   Five Big Ideas in Teaching for Mastery (NCETM, 2019)

Representation and structure

This puts great emphasis on how learners should be presented with a new concept or topic and the importance of considering different ways in which this can be achieved. Planning needs to recognise both the academic potential of the learners as well as their age, always aiming to extend learners while ensuring there is depth of understanding underpinning the ongoing development of knowledge. Internalising the learning is essential if learners are to be able to demonstrate their knowledge without requiring specific examples of concrete representation.

Mathematical thinking

Teaching for mastery includes the intention that learners will be encouraged to develop appropriate mathematical thinking skills leading to deep and sustainable learning. Learners' active involvement is essential, and teaching should include careful questioning alongside opportunities for them to discuss and explore ideas, opening up opportunities for them to reason and construct learning with guidance from the teacher. This moves away from the 'teaching by telling' model that is seen in many classrooms, asking learners to demonstrate not only their mathematical knowledge, but also their verbal and written skills, to provide explanations, conjectures and generalisations. It is important here to consider how some learners can be disadvantaged, such as those for whom English is not their first language.

Fluency

Demonstrating fluency or effective recall of mathematical procedures and concepts has always been an aim of teaching, particularly where learners are formally assessed in a summative system. For learners to demonstrate fluency in this model, there is the added intention that they will be able to use their knowledge to approach problems in different contexts and choose appropriate methods to lead to solutions. Developing fluency requires the embedding of knowledge, in most cases achieved by practice. For mastery to be developed, the aim is that this practice will include the gradual increase in complexity of the problems. McClure (2014), in an article for NRICH, discussed how practice can become a negative repetitive experience. She stressed the importance of ensuring that chosen tasks are 'in a more interesting context than usually happens'.

Variation

Variation is also sometimes referred to as intelligent practice, and – linked to the ideas around fluency – stresses the need to ensure that practice of concepts includes problems that are engaging to learners while at the same time having a direct impact on development in knowledge and understanding. Teacher planning is key here, with the emphasis on the need to represent concepts in different ways, exploring misconceptions along the way. Depth of knowledge is essential in demonstrating mastery and providing connections that encourage learners and teachers to notice and question relationships and structures.

More recently, in its introduction to professional development for secondary mathematics teachers, the NCETM has described teaching for mastery as:

> *Teaching that aims for deep and sustainable learning; learning that is rooted in an appreciation of the connectedness of mathematical ideas and based on an understanding of the underlying structures. It emphasises the need to go beyond being able to memorise facts and practise procedures and routines.*

> (NCETM, 2019)

Some misunderstandings related to mastery

The National Association of Mathematics Advisors (NAMA), an organisation that supports teacher development in mathematics, noticed an increase in the use of some aspects of a mastery approach to mathematics in schools, as well as some misunderstandings of what that approach involves. In 2015, they published *Five Myths of Mastery in Mathematics* in order to address some of these misunderstandings and clarify some of the key points.

FIVE MYTHS OF MASTERY IN MATHEMATICS (NAMA, 2015)

1. Mastery in mathematics has a single clear definition.
2. Mastery in mathematics does not allow for any differentiation.

3. There is a special curriculum which is 'the mastery curriculum'.
4. Mastery in mathematics involves repetitive practice.
5. Mastery in mathematics means you have to use particular textbooks.

It is easy to see how some of these misunderstandings about mastery might have arisen, particularly if mastery is considered to be something new and is being promoted by different organisations. Although there is no single definition of mastery, the different approaches share some common beliefs, including the fact that all learners are capable of understanding mathematical concepts and structures (NAMA, 2015). The National Curriculum has an expectation that all learners should 'move through the programmes of study at broadly the same pace' (DfE, 2014, p4), which may be responsible for the misunderstanding that mastery does not allow for differentiation. On the contrary, the National Curriculum expects that learners who understand concepts quickly will have opportunities for deeper learning, while those who take longer to understand will have opportunities to 'consolidate their understanding' (DfE, 2014, p3). The expectation that this consolidation should include additional practice may have led to the misunderstanding that teaching for mastery involves repetitive practice by learners. This misunderstanding results in the mistaken belief that learners have to practise procedures until they become fluent. The emphasis should be on carefully designed practice that develops conceptual understanding that can be applied in different contexts.

The current National Curriculum is believed to support mastery due to its aims for all learners and has been described by the NCETM (2014) as a 'mastery curriculum' (p2). However, the fact that it is content-heavy can mean that some topics are not covered in sufficient depth to be mastered by learners. There is lack of agreement in the different approaches to mastery as to what constitutes a mastery curriculum, but if learners are to achieve the depth of understanding associated with mastery, then there needs to be flexibility within the curriculum so that learners can have the time that Bloom (1968) claimed was necessary in which to do so. NAMA (2015) believes that as well as being flexible, a mastery curriculum should include 'problem solving as an integral part, aim for fluency with understanding and support development of mathematical reasoning' (p5).

Central to the delivery of an effective curriculum is the role of the teacher, their subject and pedagogic knowledge, and the tasks and questions they use to develop learners' conceptual understanding.

REFLECTIVE QUESTIONS

How would you define mastery? What does a learner need to know or be able to do in order to develop mastery in mathematics?

Historical background to mastery

Although the profile of mastery has recently been raised, it is not a new idea. According to Bloom (1973), Guskey (1980, 2007) and McCourt (2019), some of the principles and philosophies behind mastery learning date back to the works of early educators such as Comenius, Pestalozzi and Herbart, and even as far back as Aristotle. These educators shared a common belief that all learners are capable of learning well (Block and Burns, 1976; Bloom, 1973; Guskey, 1980; McCourt, 2019). The work of Washburne saw the development of a mastery approach to teaching and learning in 1920s America (Bloom, 1973; Guskey, 2007; McCourt, 2019). Washburne, according to McCourt (2019), was influenced by his experiences as a teacher in underachieving schools where only 5 per cent of learners were expected to achieve success. This was unacceptable to Washburne, as was the commonly held belief that some students were incapable of learning due to what was considered to be 'low aptitude' (McCourt, 2019, p10). Washburne was a supporter of Aristotle's approaches to teaching and sought to apply Aristotle's individual instruction approach in a group context.

McCourt (2019) describes how Washburne took up a post as superintendent of Winnetka Schools in 1919, thus enabling him to put his ideas into practice in the schools under his leadership. Central to his plan was the role of the teacher and the belief that all learners had the capacity to learn, as long as they were given sufficient time in which to do so. Washburne believed learners should be secure in what he termed the 'common essentials' before moving on to mastery (McCourt, 2019, p14), and that topics should be delivered in small, logical steps, incorporating regular assessment to check for understanding. Feedback and intervention were also key features of this approach so that any misconceptions could be addressed quickly. Washburne's mastery approach saw attainment rise in Winnetka Schools and soon became a model for effective schooling across much of the US at this time.

Carroll's work expressed an alternative view on a learner's aptitude for a subject to that commonly held at the time (Guskey, 1980). Carroll believed that learners should not be defined as either 'good' or 'poor', but more in terms of their rate of learning. He considered all learners to be capable of learning to the required level if given sufficient time. The degree to which a learner was successful was dependent on the amount of time spent understanding a topic relative to the amount of time needed by the learner to develop the required level of understanding. According to Carroll, the rate at which a learner could learn meant they were either a fast or slow learner, rather than good or poor (Guskey, 1980). Therefore, their aptitude was defined by the rate at which they learnt rather than their capacity to learn. Carroll also identified some key factors in his model for learning, namely 'perseverance' and 'opportunity to learn'. A learner's perseverance meant the amount of time they were willing to devote to a task, and an opportunity to learn referred to the time allowed in class to work on the task (Guskey, 1980, p105). Carroll also considered the 'quality of instruction' an important factor in determining the time needed to understand a topic. If this was not as effective as it should be, then more time would be needed by the learner to develop their understanding.

Benjamin Bloom (1973) was inspired by the work of both Carroll and Washburne, and developed his 'learning for mastery' approach in 1968 (Bloom, 1968, 1973; Guskey, 1980; McCourt, 2019), which was shortened to 'mastery learning', and was also based on the key belief that all learners were capable of learning if given sufficient time. This approach to 'mastery learning' meant that if sufficient time was spent developing learners' understanding of early concepts, then less time would be needed when developing later concepts because learners would have become more efficient as their mastery developed. Bloom (1973) believed that formative assessments and feedback were key features of a mastery approach to learning. Receiving precise feedback after completing short sequential units of work was seen as an important part of developing mastery in Bloom's model. If difficulties were experienced, then timely interventions could be put in place to support learners to master those concepts and achieve success before moving on to learning new concepts (Guskey, 1980; McCourt, 2019).

More recent developments of a mastery approach to teaching mathematics have emerged from East Asian countries such as Singapore and China. Results from international comparative tests (OECD, 2016; TIMSS, 2015) have seen them consistently outperform their Western counterparts in mathematics achievement. The current mathematics curriculum (DfE, 2014) was designed to reflect the key principles found in East and South East Asian countries (see Chapter 2) and to raise standards in mathematics so that most learners can achieve mastery (NCETM, 2014). To support this, the NCETM has produced the Teaching for Mastery programme to assist schools in developing mastery approaches to the teaching and learning of mathematics. The Department for Education (DfE) also funded a mathematics teacher exchange programme which was set up by the NCETM and provided opportunities for teachers to visit schools in Shanghai and host teachers from Shanghai in their schools. The purpose of these visits was to learn from practices in Shanghai and interactive teaching methods, and apply the lessons learnt to their own settings (Boylan et al., 2019). The DfE commissioned an evaluation of the programme and the extent to which Shanghai practices could be applied to schools in England. In the evaluation, Boylan (2016) discussed how schools can adopt or can adapt and develop aspects of Shanghai's approach to learning. If all or certain aspects of the approach are adopted, then success is dependent on how closely they resemble the original and on how committed the schools and teachers are to their adoption. Schools who choose to adapt and develop aspects of the Shanghai approach can select what best suits their needs and contexts. It is important to note that any changes made by schools will not result in an exact replication of the Shanghai approach to teaching due to the number of differences that exist between the countries.

In 2015, Nick Gibb (Minister of State for Schools) described mastery in mathematics as an example of one 'of the evidence-based approaches we have put at the heart of our education reforms' (Gibb, 2015), demonstrating that government officials have openly declared that there should be a move towards mastery teaching in schools. There has been an increase in the use of textbooks in schools to support the teaching of mastery, but these vary not only in their effectiveness as models of mastery, but also in how well they are used by schools. It is a mistake to think that textbooks are a necessary part of that development, and there are a number of textbook schemes available that support mastery approaches, but not one single government-recommended textbook. Boylan (2019) makes the point that adopting some of the features of a mastery approach without others will not necessarily result in a replication of achievement like that of East Asian schools. If schools choose to adopt a textbook scheme for mastery, then it is important that they have a clear understanding of the principles and practices that underpin it. Ideally, a textbook or materials created for teaching mathematics should support teachers in their planning to ensure that concepts and ideas develop as learners become increasingly mathematical in their thinking. They may also have an important role in building the confidence of teachers whose own experience of learning the subject has been procedural and 'instrumental' (Skemp, 1976). High-quality textbooks can provide a useful resource to support teachers in the classroom, but even the best textbook will prove ineffective if used by a teacher who lacks understanding in the principles and practices of a mastery approach to teaching and learning. This identifies the need to recognise some of the theory behind the mastery approach.

Theoretical exploration of mastery

The NCETM (2016b) set out a number of ideas that sit behind their curriculum model. The first of these suggests that 'Maths teaching for mastery rejects the idea that a large proportion of people "just can't do maths"'. This supports the view of Guskey and Gates (1986), who suggested that 'all children can learn when provided with appropriate conditions for their learning' (p73).

The second premise from the NCETM (2016b) suggests that 'All pupils are encouraged by belief that by working hard at maths they can succeed'. This supports Dweck's (1999) point that learners who believed intelligence was not fixed, and whose aim was to learn as much as they could, were more successful. Skemp (1976) made it clear that 'relational' understanding, where students are encouraged to connect learning, is more effective than 'instrumental' understanding, where memory and rote learning are predominant. With these factors in mind, a mastery curriculum is aimed at providing both the opportunities to consider patterns and generalisations individually and, as Vygotsky (1978) suggested with his notion of the zone of proximal development, for learners to engage in the important process of discussion and shared learning. Mason and Johnston-Wilder (2006) linked this to ideas considering learner engagement and their behaviour in the learning situation. The 'asserting mode' suggested encourages learners to question and 'take the initiative' (Mason and Johnston-Wilder, 2006, p2), which sits well with the style of lesson described in the mastery model. The focusing of lessons on one aspect of the subject was explored by Denvir and Brown (1986) when they were considering the learning experiences of lower-attaining students. The emphasis is that learning mathematics is not a linear process, and so by immersing learners in explorative tasks, aiming for deeper understanding, all students are supported and unexpected learning can occur.

Recognising the role of assessment in the teaching and learning of mathematics has always been essential when curriculum models are considered. As Newell (2017) points out, 'the content of national testing directly affects what is taught' (p4). This has always been relevant in the research into learning theories associated with mathematics. Boaler (1997) suggested that learners who learn mathematics through open-ended exploration and problem-solving perform better in assessments than similar learners who have been taught using methods that focus around techniques and algorithms.

The idea that ability in mathematics is not fixed is essential to the mastery teaching approach, where learning develops alongside the building of links between concepts or 'pockets of subject knowledge' (Newell, 2017, p9). Learning theories proposed over a number of years support the importance of recognising this.

Central to the NCETM's description is the need to ensure that learners are fully supported. Therefore, the importance of 'lesson design' that considers the sequencing of learning is highlighted. Included in this is the need to consider in advance where misconceptions may occur, as well as any interventions that may be required. The selection of appropriate tasks and clarity around how these are presented to learners is also an essential component of planning for effective mathematical learning activities.

This is explored by Mason and Johnston-Wilder (2006) when they state that 'interactions need purpose and context' (p13).

While a focus of mastery learning emphasises the need for exploration and deep understanding, there is also a place for considering how memorising facts that form the basis of the subject can be important. As Watson et al. (2003) suggest, 'memory for what is important needs explicit work' (p26), and again this forms a component of the designing of lessons. Consideration of how this impacts on the aim 'to avoid cognitive overload in the working memory and enable pupils to focus on new concepts' (NCETM, 2016b) needs to be recognised as important, but should not be the only approach that learners are encouraged to adopt if they are to develop deep structures for their mathematical knowledge.

Mastery in different settings

Primary settings

The expectation in primary settings is that most schools will follow the National Curriculum guidance for teaching mathematics, which is statutory for state and voluntary-aided schools (DfE, 2014). Although there are no official government recommendations, an increasing number of schools are adopting, with varying degrees of success, mathematics schemes that are centred around specific textbooks. University tutors for student teachers on school placements have observed how mastery is understood and how it is interpreted and taught in some schools. In order to gain a wider picture of how schools perceive mastery, data were collected from final-year student teachers regarding their experiences of mastery in schools in and around London. The questions are listed in Chapter 8, but those being focused on here relate to whether mastery was being discussed in schools, if it was seen in practice, and what it looked like.

Out of 31 student teachers questioned, 13 saw little or no mention of mastery in schools. The responses of those who had heard it mentioned included hearing about it at staff meetings, as a challenge for higher-attaining learners or when referring to a 'mastery scheme'. One student teacher experienced it being incorporated within lessons across the curriculum and four saw it as part of the structure of lessons or questions used by the teacher. When asked to describe what mastery looked like in practice, 17 respondents experienced it as extension activities, an out-of-class club for higher-achieving learners, or where higher-achieving learners supported those who were not achieving as well. Seven responses included observing mastery as consolidating learning or explaining reasoning. One respondent, whose school followed a 'mastery scheme', rarely observed mastery in practice because, according to her class teacher, 'the children were deemed to be unable to access mastery'.

It is quite clear from the responses of the 31 student teachers that their experiences of mastery in schools differed considerably. Other differences included how different textbooks and resources were used and with which year groups. Some schools followed them strictly, while others were more selective depending on the class teacher's subject knowledge and the availability of resources. With three different placements to complete, student teachers on the three-year undergraduate teacher training programme can experience different approaches to mastery and different interpretations, potentially causing confusion. Boylan (2019) discusses the difficulties teachers and schools face when trying to get a clear understanding of the meaning of mastery in mathematics, which is not helped by the different 'mastery schemes' and textbooks available.

The responses from student teachers as well as university tutors' experiences in schools indicate that there is a lack of consistency not only in understanding what is meant by mastery in mathematics, but also how to teach for mastery in primary settings. Schools where approaches are effective and develop learners' deeper conceptual understanding have a shared understanding and the support of senior leaders, who have invested time and money in staff development and the acquisition of effective resources. The development of mastery in mathematics is less effective in schools where textbook schemes are followed strictly without deviation and where little or no training is provided on the principles and practices involved in this approach.

Secondary settings

In the secondary mathematics classroom, it has been common to adopt a spiral curriculum model, where learners revisit topics regularly to reinforce and consolidate learning. This traditional curriculum model has been common practice for at least 50 years, promoted by Bruner (1960), who believed that 'a curriculum as it develops should revisit these basic ideas repeatedly, building upon them until the student has grasped the full formal apparatus that goes with them' (p13).

Curriculum design has focused on planning schemes of work and teaching routines around this idea, moving learners on to the next topic based on a planned set of timings rather than on their ability to demonstrate understanding of the concepts. The focus on revisiting topics, often with long gaps in between, has resulted in learners repeating areas of the mathematics curriculum without necessarily encountering new concepts or ideas. The role of support materials such as textbooks has been important in advocating this model of teaching, breaking topics down into 'chapter-sized' chunks of learning without considering the links to higher-level aspects of a topic. However, it is interesting to recognise that Nick Gibb (Minister of State for Schools) has supported the use of textbooks, provided they are of a 'high standard', in his foreword to a policy paper by Tim Oates (2014).

In order to move this to a mastery model, the curriculum would need to allow for more depth and structure to be planned into each lesson. This has its own challenges in the secondary environment, not least of which is the shortage of qualified and experienced classroom practitioners with the specialist mathematical knowledge and confidence to work in a different way. Figures from the Labour Party from 2017 identify over 600,000 learners in England being taught by unqualified teachers (Syal, 2017). Based on this, there are likely to be numerous occasions when learners' mathematics lessons are taught by a teacher who is not fluent with the ideas behind teaching for mastery. The level of teaching competency required to 'focus on both procedural/factual fluency and conceptual understanding' (ASCL, n.d.) needs to be recognised both in terms of the day-to-day classroom situation and the longer-term overview of how the curriculum is structured.

For a mastery curriculum model to be in place, there is a need to review the existing curriculum and redesign and resource it appropriately. As mentioned previously, textbooks play a large part in this. Within secondary schools, there are already a substantial number of textbooks available to select from, varying in quality. Schools will be reluctant to invest in new materials, even if these were readily available for secondary teaching, unless they can be certain that the outcomes of using them will enhance the attainment of learners. Alongside this has been the drive in schools to move to the use of digital resources for teaching. Teachers who are prepared to engage with the idea of mastery learning will need to sift through the content of both the digital and paper versions of materials available to them as part of their planning process, which, of course, also brings into play the issues of workload and provision of planning time.

The curriculum design associated with mastery learning also requires a change in the approaches to planning and delivery. In Shanghai, it is traditional for teachers to plan together and to aim this planning at ensuring that all learners reach a similar point by the end of the lesson. Traditionally, setting of learners for mathematics in secondary schools places learners in subclasses according to their attainment, and this in turn leads to planning, which recognises the narrowed range of abilities within the group. The Singapore approach places less emphasis on differentiation by task or content and largely avoids in-class grouping by prior attainment (Micklewright et al., 2014). In this situation, there is a greater emphasis on planning the lesson to accommodate all of the mathematical attainers with the class, aligning more to the concept of mixed-ability teaching that is more common in primary schools. If one aim of the lesson is to keep learners working together, then there needs to be a focus in the planning on ensuring that learners who grasp concepts quickly continue to be challenged by complex problems while simultaneously supporting the lower-attaining students to build their understanding with additional practice.

REFLECTIVE QUESTIONS

What does mastery look like in your setting? How could you develop a more holistic approach to teaching for mastery? How can you ensure that mastery teaching and learning is sustainable in your setting?

CHAPTER SUMMARY

Key points covered in this chapter are:

- mastery in teaching and learning mathematics is not new, and some of the underpinning principles and philosophies have been in existence since the teachings of Aristotle and other early educators;
- a shared feature of all interpretations and approaches to mastery in mathematics is the belief that all learners can be successful if they are given sufficient time in which to develop their understanding;
- learners must be given opportunities to develop conceptual understanding and procedural fluency through the use of a variety of resources and representations and a carefully designed curriculum.

Further reading

Haylock, D. (2019) *Mathematics Explained for Primary Teachers*, 6th edn. London: SAGE.

This is a useful book for beginner and early career teachers who wish to improve their mathematics subject and pedagogical knowledge.

Drury, H. (2018) *How to Teach Mathematics for Mastery*. Oxford: Oxford University Press.

Although aimed at secondary teachers, this book also has relevance for primary colleagues and makes some key points with regard to mastering mathematics in any setting.

McCourt, M. (2019) *Teaching for Mastery*. Woodbridge: John Catt Educational.

This book gives an outline of the history of mastery learning and teaching as it developed from the ideas of early educators such as Carroll and Bloom.

References

Association of School and College Leaders (ASCL) (n.d.) *ASCL Guidance: Mathematics Teaching for Mastery*. Available at: https://tonystephens.org.uk/download/%20subject_related_documents/misc_documents/guidance_paper_maths_teaching_for_mastery__jan_2016.pdf

Block, J. and Burns, R. (1976) 'Mastery learning'. *Review of Research in Education*, 4(1): 3–49.

Bloom, B.S. (1968) 'Learning for mastery'. *Evaluation Comment*, 1(2): 1–12.

Bloom, B.S. (1973) 'Recent developments in mastery learning'. *Educational Psychologist*, 10(2): 53–7.

Boaler, J. (1997) *Experiencing School Mathematics: Teaching Styles, Sex, and Setting*. Buckingham: Open University Press.

Boylan, M. (2016) 'Developing frameworks for evaluating and researching the Shanghai Mathematics Teacher Exchange: practices or assemblage'. In G. Adams (ed.), *Proceedings of the British Society for Research into Learning Mathematics*, 36(2): 13–18.

Boylan, M. (2019) 'Remastering mathematics: mastery, remixes and mash ups'. *Mathematics Teaching*, 266: 14–18.

Boylan, M., Wolstenholme, C., Demack, S., Maxwell, B., Jay, T., Adams, G. and Reaney, S. (2019) *Longitudinal Evaluation of the Mathematics Teacher Exchange: China–England – Final Report*. London: DfE.

Bruner, J. (1960) *The Process of Education*. Cambridge, MA: Harvard University Press.

Collins English Dictionary (2006) Glasgow: HarperCollins.

Denvir, B. and Brown, M. (1986) 'Understanding number concepts in low attaining 7–9 year olds'. *Educational Studies in Mathematics*, 17(1): 15–36.

Department for Education (DfE) (2014) *National Curriculum in England: Mathematics Programme of Study*. Available at: www.gov.uk/government/publications/national-curriculum-in-england-mathematics-programmes-of-study/national-curriculum-in-england-mathematics-programmes-of-study

Department of Education and Science (DES) and Welsh Office (1989) *Mathematics in the National Curriculum*. London: HMSO.

Dweck, C.S. (1999) *Self-Theories: Their Role in Motivation, Personality and Development*. Philadelphia, PA: Psychology Press.

Gibb, N. (2015) *Speech on Government's Mathematics Reforms*. Available at: www.gov.uk/government/speeches/nick-gibb-speech-on-governments-maths-reforms

Guskey, T.R. (1980) 'Mastery learning: applying the theory'. *Theory into Practice*, 19(2): 104–11.

Guskey, T.R. (2007) 'Closing achievement gaps: revisiting Benjamin S. Bloom's "Learning for Mastery"'. *Journal of Advanced Academics*, 19(1): 8–31.

Guskey, T.R. and Gates, S.L. (1986) 'Synthesis of research on the effects of mastery learning in elementary and secondary classrooms'. *Educational Leadership*, 43(8): 72–80.

Haylock, D. and Cockburn, A. (2017) *Understanding Mathematics for Young Children*. London: SAGE.

Mason, J. and Johnston-Wilder, S. (2006) *Designing and Using Mathematical Tasks*, 2nd edn. St Albans: Tarquin/Open University.

Mathematics Mastery (2019) *The Mathematics Mastery Primary Programme*. Available at: www.mathematicsmastery.org/primary-programme-teacher-training-classroom-resources

McClure, L. (2014) *Developing Number Fluency: What, Why and How*. Available at: https://nrich.maths.org/10624

McCourt, M. (2019) *Teaching for Mastery*. Woodbridge: John Catt Educational.

Micklewright, J., Jerrim, J., Vignoles, A., Jenkins, A., Allen, R., Ilie, S. and Hein, C. (2014) *Teachers in England's Secondary Schools: Evidence from TALIS 2013*. Available at: https://assets.publishing.service.gov.uk/government/uploads/system/uploads/attachment_data/file/322910/RR302_-_TALIS_report_NC.pdf

National Association of Mathematics Advisors (NAMA) (2015) *Five Myths of Mastery in Mathematics*. Available at: www.nama.org.uk/Downloads/Five%20Myths%20about%20Mathematics%20Mastery.pdf

National Centre for Excellence in the Teaching of Mathematics (NCETM) (2014) *Mastery Approaches to Mathematics and the New National Curriculum*. Available at: www.ncetm.org.uk/public/files/19990433

National Centre for Excellence in the Teaching of Mathematics (NCETM) (2016a) *Mastery Explained*. Available at: www.ncetm.org.uk/resources/49450

National Centre for Excellence in the Teaching of Mathematics (NCETM) (2016b) *The Essence of Maths Teaching for Mastery*. Available at: www.ncetm.org.uk/files/37086535/The+Essence+of+Maths+Teaching+for+Mastery+june+2016.pdf

National Centre for Excellence in the Teaching of Mathematics (NCETM) (2019) *Five Big Ideas in Teaching for Mastery*. Available at: www.ncetm.org.uk/resources/50042

Newell, R. (2017) *Big Ideas in Primary Mathematics*. London: SAGE.

Nunes, T. and Bryant, P. (1998) *Children Doing Mathematics*. Oxford: Blackwell.

Oates, T. (2014) *Why Textbooks Count: A Policy Paper*. Available at: www.cambridgeassessment.org.uk/Images/181744-why-textbooks-count-tim-oates.pdf

Organisation for Economic Co-operation and Development (OECD) (2016) *PISA 2015 Results (Volume 1): Excellence and Equity in Education*. Available at: https://read.oecd-ilibrary.org/education/pisa-2015-results-volume-i_9789264266490-en#page180

Skemp, R.R. (1976) 'Relational understanding and instrumental understanding'. *Mathematics Teaching*, 77: 20–6.

Syal, R. (2017) 'More than 600,000 pupils in England taught by unqualified teachers, says Labour'. *The Guardian*, 25 July.

Trends in International Mathematics and Science Study (TIMSS) (2015) *International Mathematics Achievement*. Available at: http://timssandpirls.bc.edu/timss2015/international-results/timss-2015/mathematics/student-achievement/

Vignoles, A., Jerrim, J. and Cowan, R. (2015) *Mathematics Mastery Primary Evaluation Report*. London: Education Endowment Fund.

Vygotsky, L.S. (1978) *Mind in Society: The Development of the Higher Psychological Processes*. London: Harvard University Press.

Watson, A., De Geest, E. and Prestage, S. (2003) *Deep Progress in Mathematics: The Improving Attainment in Mathematics Project*. Oxford: University of Oxford Department of Educational Studies.

2

DEVELOPMENTAL SIDE OF MASTERY: CONCEPTUAL UNDERSTANDING

LOUISE HOSKYNS-STAPLES

KEYWORDS: CONCEPTUAL UNDERSTANDING; CURRICULUM AIMS; INTERVENTION; KNOWING VERSUS UNDERSTANDING; MATHEMATICAL PROFICIENCY; MATHEMATICAL STRUCTURE; METACOGNITION; VARIATION THEORY

CHAPTER OBJECTIVES

This chapter will allow you to achieve the following outcomes:

- unpick the key ideas in teaching for conceptual understanding;
- see how conceptual understanding fits within the development of mathematical proficiency;
- develop an understanding of metacognition;
- look at how appropriate it is to keep learners together for their learning while addressing the needs of individual learners;
- explore how to challenge and support learners when they are all learning at the same pace.

Introduction

A basic task is to determine what is meant by mastery of the subject and to search for methods and materials which will enable the largest proportion of students to attain such mastery.

(Bloom, 1968, p1)

This chapter will look at what is meant by mastery in an English classroom with particular emphasis on developing an understanding of the mathematical concepts that are taught. The English mathematics National Curriculum emphasises conceptual understanding within the first of its three key aims for mathematics learning and teaching: 'become fluent in … mathematics … so that pupils develop conceptual understanding and the ability to recall and apply knowledge rapidly and accurately' (DfE, 2013, p3). We will establish what makes a curriculum a mastery curriculum and look at how this supports developmental learning.

Multiple definitions of mastery exist, which can make it difficult for teachers to decide how to approach this pedagogy (NAMA, 2016; Rycroft-Smith and Boylan, 2019). The origins of the approach can be traced back to the work of Bloom (1968) and Carroll (1970). Bearing this in mind, this chapter attempts to address the commonalities of these approaches outlined by NAMA (2016), such as keeping the whole class together, spending enough time on material so that it is understood, and enabling conceptual understanding through multiple representations (conceptual variation).

The pedagogical approach required to develop conceptual understanding, a key part of a mathematics mastery curriculum, will be explored here, followed by looking at how conceptual understanding fits within mathematical proficiency. Overall, the chapter will consider why it is important to understand the mathematics behind the procedures that learners need to use.

REFLECTIVE QUESTION

Mathematics is a conceptual subject, but what does that mean in practice?

Mastery learning adapted to an English classroom

When we talk about mastery in the context of mathematics, what do we actually mean?

There is a difference between knowing something and understanding it; for example, a child may know the order of the numbers to 10 and be able to recite 1, 2, 3, 4, 5, …, 10, but cannot yet count a set of objects as he or she does not know what the numbers mean. Mathematics can be thought of as knowing lots of facts; for example, 360° around a point or $3 \times 5 = 15$. When teaching for mastery, we are looking for long-term understanding rather than merely knowing.

Common to definitions of mastery is the focus on developing a conceptual understanding of the mathematics alongside procedural knowledge and memorisation. This will lead to mastery as learners will be able to apply their knowledge to new or unfamiliar situations or solve new problems in unfamiliar situations (Drury, 2015, p9).

Mastery learning as developed by Bloom (1968) and Carroll (1970) has some distinctive features that are present in the mastery approaches employed in current-day English classrooms:

- time is provided to ensure that all learners master the content;

- a belief that once something is learnt well, that learning is retained;

- assessment is used to inform the teaching rather than purely to assign a grade or level;

- the group of learners is kept together;

- a belief that effective planning and teaching strategies will enable all learners to achieve; and

- learners should develop perseverance when faced with challenge.

Bloom's (1968) belief that the vast majority of learners have the potential to master topics given enough time has strong implications for our classroom practice and is reflected in the English National Curriculum, which states, 'the expectation is that the majority of pupils will move through the programmes of study at broadly the same pace' (DfE, 2013, p3). There is no expectation, however, that learners all complete the same work; the curriculum expectation is that support is provided to those who are learning the material more slowly and that others are provided with rich and sophisticated problems. To enable this, time needs to be found to ensure that slower learners can understand and master the content appropriately.

Providing enough time for learners to achieve and embed the learning

A mastery curriculum has the expectation that learners have mastered the curriculum before moving on to a new topic, so inevitably longer needs to be spent teaching and practising the material to ensure that learners have developed a deep and long-lasting understanding. Learners need to be given the time to accommodate the new ideas, conceptualise them and find the connections with prior learning. To achieve this, learning needs to be carefully orchestrated so that understanding of the concept is developed alongside the ability to use the mathematical tools. Once the skill has been learnt, time needs to be given to embed the learning through both practice and application (Drury, 2015). If learners move on too quickly, the skill that they have just about learnt will be lost as that learning is replaced by the new learning. Learning new skills requires the brain to make new links and takes time; learners then need to use that skill to ensure that it is learnt deeply, fully understood, and the links created in the brain are kept (Boaler, 2016). An analogy that is commonly used is that of a musician learning a piece of music; this is a process that takes time, effort and determination, as well as the belief that the hard work will result in success. Once the piece is learnt, the musician then practises the piece and can begin experimenting with clear aims for what they want to achieve. It is this extended practice that embeds the learning and makes that learning sustainable for the long term.

Careful planning and effective strategies to enable all learners to achieve

Bloom (1968, p1) highlighted the need for attention to be paid to the preparation of lessons, stating that teachers should 'search for methods and materials' to enable learners to master the content. Enabling learners to understand the mathematics they are being taught rather than purely completing an exercise requires careful attention to the lesson structure and the material provided. Lessons need to be developmentally appropriate, enabling learners to bridge the gap between what they already know and the learning that is provided (Vygotsky, 2011). Planning for misconceptions and common errors can further support children in developing a rounded understanding of a concept. If learners are also kept together, then it is essential to establish what learning is appropriate at a particular age and stage of development (age-related expectations). Many jurisdictions facilitate this for educators through providing teacher guidance in the form of a National Curriculum.

REFLECTIVE QUESTION

As long as learners can get the right answer, does it matter if they understand how they got there?

RESEARCH

The development of fluency in the curriculum

The 2014 revision of the National Curriculum was informed by a review of the curricula of five high-performing jurisdictions. Clear aims for the curricula were found in each of the high-performing jurisdictions, and this was a recommendation for the new English curriculum. These aims were broadly:

- developing fluency that is underpinned by conceptual understanding;
- solving unfamiliar problems;
- reasoning mathematically to present an argument using mathematical language; and
- developing a positive disposition.

These first three aims are reflected in the 2014 English curriculum, and – as we have seen above – part of the idea of mastery is the belief that all children can achieve mathematically, given enough time. The final aim forms part of a mastery curriculum and will be explored in greater depth in the section on mathematical proficiency. The review also noted that in Singapore, emphasis was placed on *mastering* the content of each particular year prior to moving forwards, with an explicit emphasis on factual, procedural and conceptual knowledge. The review found that this is supported by a growing body of research analysing the relationship between the three aspects of learning, which found that all are 'important and mutually reinforce each other … a combination of all of these processes is required for pupils to become adaptable mathematical problem solvers' (DfE, 2012, pp65-7). The government particularly wanted to emphasise fluency, which was initially interpreted by some as mechanistic learning, but Stefano Pozzi (2013, p2), who played a key role in overseeing the curriculum, affirmed that fluency does not equate to rote learning, conceptual understanding is to be valued, and practice needs to provide opportunities to achieve that understanding. A report into the teaching of mathematics in schools in England and Wales (commonly referred to as the Cockcroft Report after the author) made this point clearly: 'We need to distinguish between "fluent" performance and "mechanical" performance. Fluent performance is based on understanding of the routine which is being carried out; mechanical performance is performance by rote in which the necessary understanding is not present' (Cockcroft, 1982, p239).

Prior to adopting a new approach to teaching, it is essential to evaluate the evidence that this approach can be successful in a local setting rather than simply adopting a pedagogy developed elsewhere, and this has been done to a limited extent. Most recently, the England–China mathematics teacher exchange was evaluated by Boylan et al. (2019) on behalf of the English Department for Education (DfE) to assess the impact on learners' attainment from teacher visits to Shanghai. The report found very limited evidence of higher attainment in Key Stage 1 (5–7-year-olds) and little or no impact in older children. It was noted that the exchange had informed the teaching for mastery approach adopted by the NCETM and that schools had implemented the approach in lower school years initially, then continued with it as learners moved through the school, so the impact would be lower on upper primary years. In contrast, a report evaluating the impact of the textbook series *Inspire Maths*, the UK edition of the Singaporean *My Pals Are Here!* series, by Hall et al. (2016) found that Year 1 children (5–6-year-olds) had made 'a small but significant amount of extra progress' (p5). This evidence supports the earlier findings of Jerrim and Vignoles (2015), who conducted two trials in Ark schools that had implemented mathematics mastery, an adapted form of the Singapore approach, for one year. They found that the mastery approach had a 'modest but positive' effect on learners (p6). A stated aim of the Ark mathematics mastery curriculum was to 'dramatically shift national expectations … and to ensure that every single child meets them and that many excel' (Drury, 2015, p4). This belief that all children can and should succeed is also a key tenet of the NCETM mastery programme: 'Mastery is characterised by a belief that, by working hard, all children are capable of succeeding at mathematics. On this basis, children are taught all together as a class and are not split into "prior attainment" groupings' (NCETM, 2017).

REFLECTIVE QUESTION

The English mathematics National Curriculum has clearly stated aims. How do they influence the mathematics learnt in the classroom?

Success in mathematics for all learners

In this section, we will look at what enables learners to be successful, what is meant by mathematical proficiency, and how this supports learners to develop a deep and lasting understanding of mathematics.

What is a mathematical concept?

Before considering conceptual understanding, we need to consider what we actually mean by a concept. The *Oxford Encyclopedic English Dictionary* (1991) definition is 'an idea or mental picture of a group or class of objects formed by combining all their aspects' (p302). Another definition that is also given is 'an abstract idea' (p302). So, by collecting together our thoughts about a group of objects, we can form an abstract idea.

Using the example of a tree, consider how a child learns about the concept of trees. There are deciduous trees and evergreens, both quite different, so over time the child draws together the group of objects until the abstract idea of a tree is formed. Alongside this drawing together of similar members of the group, the child also has to learn which objects do not belong to the group 'trees' although they possess similarities. This idea can then be extended to other objects that follow a similar structure but are not trees. So, a learner needs to be able to differentiate between what is and what is not part of the concept (Forgasz and Leder, 2008). The contrast between an object that belongs to the concept and one that does not enables learners to bring out the characteristics of the first object. Through differentiation that becomes more sophisticated over time, learners refine their definition. For example, why is a large shrub not called a tree? Both have leaves, both are made of wood, both have branches; the difference is that shrubs have multiple stems. Making changes to certain mathematical features to draw learners' attention to the structure of the concept is discussed in greater detail below in the section on variation.

Generalisation and misconceptions

A mastery pedagogy seeks to develop a deep conceptual understanding so that learners can generalise, find patterns and justify their reasoning (Drury, 2015). The process of generalisation and abstraction is an essential part of learning and is a consequence of noticing what is happening, spotting patterns and drawing conclusions from repeated behaviour. Part of constructing mathematical knowledge is to systematically generalise from the experiences provided as part of learning, but this can lead to misconceptions or partly formed (naive) conceptions through under- or overgeneralisation. A misconception is different from an error as an error is a mistake that is made at surface level rather than a misunderstanding of a concept (Hansen et al., 2017). Sometimes learners overgeneralise; a commonly cited example of this is that the multiplication of a number by 10 involves adding a zero to the end of the number (e.g. $8 \times 10 = 80$), so in later education learners make the mistake that $3.8 \times 10 = 3.80$. Exploring and highlighting misconceptions can bring them out into the open as they are common to all learners and also support learners in re-conceptualising the mathematics (Drury, 2015; Hansen et al., 2017). Dealing with misconceptions through teaching them explicitly is part of the mastery approach (and many other pedagogical approaches) to enable them to be rapidly addressed (NAMA, 2016) and provide learning for the whole class. The National Curriculum states that 'children should use discussion to probe and remedy their misconceptions' (DfE, 2013, p4).

Variation theory

By keeping some elements the same, it is easier to establish what is different, which helps the learner to develop a deeper understanding of a concept. Maria Montessori (cited in Forgasz and

Leder, 2008, p156) was interested in the training of the senses by systematic variation against an invariant background. Dienes' third principle of mathematics learning, the mathematical variability principle, states that concepts should be learnt by varying the maximum number of variables possible (Gu et al., 2004). Cockcroft (1982, paras 238–9) discusses the need for some mathematical facts and knowledge to be 'learnt by heart' but rejects the premise that this should be achieved by rote drilling without developing an understanding of the mathematics related to the facts. The report also advocates practice to develop fluency. Variation allows large groups of learners to achieve meaningful learning and avoids the need for learning by rote as the relationships between the different options given allow learners to generate their own new knowledge rather than relying on memorisation (Gu et al., 2004, p342; Kilpatrick et al., 2001). Cuoco et al. (1996) develop this idea further:

- encouraging teachers to allow their learners to be 'experimenters', systematically changing one variable at a time;

- 'visualisers', constructing a picture of a concept in various ways; and

- 'tinkerers', who take ideas apart and put them back together in a different way.

Bloom (1984) described mastery learning as 'improving the students' learning from the same teaching over a series of learning tasks' (p7).

Applying these theories to our idea of a tree: trees have a wooden trunk, this is invariant – it does not change; trees have leaves, this is variable – some have broad leaves, some have pine needles, and so on. Learners picture the concept in a range of different ways. Given enough time, the child makes connections between all the different, unconnected objects, is able to find the similarities despite the obvious differences, and generalises from this to form the abstract idea of a tree. Eventually, that abstraction can even encompass a Japanese art form, the bonsai.

Bruner's (1966) ideas of discovery learning form part of the mastery approach. Bruner discussed learning in three interrelated stages: (1) enactive, when a learner can touch and feel; (2) iconic, when a learner recognises the image of the object; and (3) symbolic, when a learner recognises that something can be represented by something else. The concrete–pictorial–abstract (CPA) approach, informed by Bruner's enactive–iconic–symbolic stages of learning (Hoong et al., 2015), is a method of developing understanding of a mathematical concept by varying the representation of the mathematics by using apparatus, a diagram or sketch, or an abstract method; for example, to develop an understanding of square numbers, a learner can create square arrays with pegs or counters, draw squares on dotted paper, or multiply a number by itself and find the total. Through these experiences, the learner develops an understanding of the concept of square numbers rather than merely rote learning the answer to 8^2. Again, this is not a new approach; we have long used a range of methods to find solutions for equations. For example, for $y = 2x + 3$, traditionally a learner could plot a graph (pictorial) or solve the equation algebraically (abstract). The learner could also use Cuisenaire rods or cubes (concrete materials) to model the graph (see Figure 2.1) or to deepen their understanding further by creating their own problem involving the equation.

The idea of representing the mathematics in multiple ways has been incorporated into the mastery approach: 'a concept … has been *mastered* when a person can represent it in multiple ways … and can think mathematically with the concept' (Drury, 2015, p9, emphasis in original).

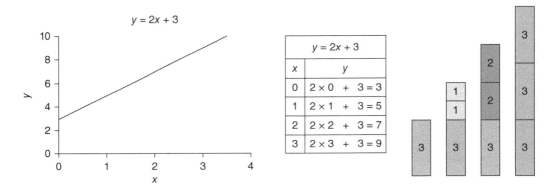

Figure 2.1   *y = 2x + 3 represented graphically, algebraically and with Cuisenaire rods*

Gu et al. (2004) discuss two different ways to vary mathematics to enable learners to better understand the structure of the mathematics: conceptual variation by presenting a concept from multiple perspectives, discussed above, and procedural variation through solving problems to clarify the critical points. Building on the example given in Figure 2.1, learners could plot $y = 2x + c$, using different values of c, such as 1, 0 and −2; the aim being to choose values and representations carefully to support the learner in noticing the effect of the changes (see Figure 2.2). The right-hand equation includes the example where $m = 0$ to draw learners' attention to this option.

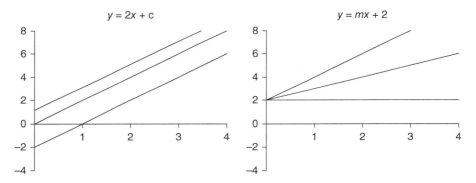

Figure 2.2   *The graphs of y = mx + c varying c and then varying m*

Giving learners examples such as this enables them to see the changes in the line generated by only changing one constant each time. Both types of variation enable learners to develop a deeper conceptual understanding of the mathematics. The role of the teacher here is to support the learner in noticing what is happening.

Five strands of mathematical proficiency

Conceptual understanding and procedural knowledge are two of the five strands of mathematical proficiency explored by Kilpatrick et al. (2001), who were interested in promoting particular cognitive changes in learners to enable their success in mathematics. This led to a definition of mathematical proficiency as a blend of the following five interwoven skills rather than a single approach:

- conceptual understanding (the comprehension of mathematical concepts);

- procedural fluency (the skill of being able to carry out procedures flexibly and appropriately);

- strategic competence (the ability to formulate and solve problems);

- adaptive reasoning (the capacity for logical thought, explanation and justification); and

- a productive disposition (the inclination to see that mathematics is useful and a belief that the learner can be successful).

(pp116–17)

Kilpatrick et al. (2001) note that attending to one or two strands at the expense of the others will not be effective in achieving proficiency. These five strands are reminiscent of the aims of the curricula discussed above and are also reflected in the mastery approach. Much has been written and said about a growth mindset (Boaler, 2013; Rattan et al., 2012; Stripp, 2014) and the fact that viewing intelligence as fixed can cause learners who struggle to have little belief in their own ability to achieve (self-efficacy). By teaching the whole class together and the teacher making the assumption that all learners can achieve, learners have a much greater chance of developing a productive disposition.

Intervention in a mastery context

Bloom's mastery learning has been shown to be an effective pedagogical approach, particularly for struggling learners (Guskey, 2010; NAMA, 2016; Trundley et al., 2017), due to the additional time that is provided and the immediacy of the remedial teaching provided.

Providing for the range of needs of learners to support all of them in the development of mathematical proficiency while keeping the class together could easily look like a daunting prospect. Carroll (1970) believed that aptitude was the amount of time needed by a learner to attain mastery of a task, and that the relationship between the time spent learning and the time needed could be given by:

$$\text{degree of learning} = \frac{\text{time spent}}{\text{time needed}}$$

Bearing this in mind, as well as the view that the vast majority of learners can achieve, leads to the inevitable need for more time to be provided for these learners in the school day. The alternative to remedial work after a lesson is to pre-teach vulnerable learners the key skills required to grasp the concept prior to that learning taking place in a whole-class situation. Trundley et al. (2017), in a year-long project, looked at pre-teaching and assigning competence as an alternative to supporting children after the lesson. A major difference between the pre- and post-teaching methods was that pre-teaching significantly increased learners' confidence and self-efficacy: 'Children who had no belief in themselves as learners in mathematics now believe in themselves, and are actively involved in their own learning and in the learning of others' (Trundley et al., 2017, p3).

Since 2017, the NCETM has run a national teacher research group project based around intervention in a mastery context, aiming to move from the traditional catch-up model to the keep-up model advocated in a mastery pedagogy. Over 400 teachers explored possible approaches to keeping the class together, such as pre-teaching or same-day intervention (post-teaching).

Case studies were conducted over the academic year to inform teacher practice. The common findings across the different projects were that an increase in engagement and confidence was seen in the learners (productive disposition). More specific findings were that post-teaching enabled children to keep up with the class so that they could access the learning in the following lesson. Unlike traditional intervention, the learners were not always the same, although there were some who needed input more regularly. Pre-teaching enabled learners who normally lacked confidence in their own mathematical ability to actively participate with confidence in the lesson prior to failing, corroborating the findings of Trundley et al. (2017). Learners who were significantly behind still needed other more structured forms of intervention.

What does it mean to have 'mastered' a concept?

Learners have a wide range of aptitudes and experiences that impact on how they approach the mathematics taught in school. Some children absorb information rapidly and need additional challenges to support their development and enjoyment of mathematics. If we look at the programmes of study set out in the curriculum, there will be some children who exceed them before the start of the year. Taking an extreme example of a child who begins school at 4 years old already knowing all the multiplication facts to 12, can we say that the child has mastered multiplication? We may think it is fair to assert that the child has 'mastered' the multiplication facts, but without an assessment of understanding a teacher cannot know whether the child can apply the facts or relate them to other concepts. Would the child know the answer to a contextual question, such as: How many boots do three children need to go to forest school?

Questions to ask might be:

- How many children are there?

- How many boots does each child need?

- How many boots do they need altogether?

This is an activity that all the learners in the class can engage in and use different mathematics to be successful. The answers could be achieved through touching and counting each object (embedding the one-to-one principle of counting), counting aloud in ones without touching, and counting in twos. If a child, such as the 4-year-old described above, can link the 'story' to the known fact, $2 \times 3 = 6$, this would demonstrate that this knowledge can be applied.

Figure 2.3 shows some ideas for playing with classroom materials to support the development of the understanding behind the learnt facts; for example, making stars using five sticks for each star. The teacher can pose questions to establish understanding; for example, if the child has made two stars, asking how many sticks are needed for three stars, and so on. Another example could be: How many different equal groups can be made from 12 counters? Asking what is the same about each group and what is different will enable the teacher to see if the child knows that the total will always be 12 or if counting was required each time, assessing conservation of number. Tasks such as these will develop the conceptual understanding required for future connected learning. Exploring options such as 'How many different groups can you make?' or 'Have you found all the ways?' followed by 'How do you know?' or 'Are you sure?' can extend and embed learning without moving to harder material.

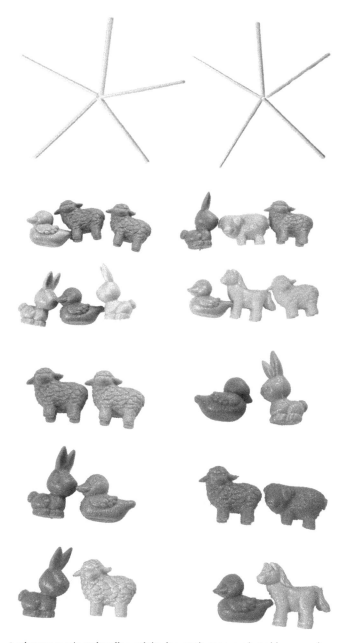

Figure 2.3   A picture made using five sticks for each star, and making equal groups from 12 counters

Could the child draw a story that shows multiplication? This would provide a creative challenge that really demonstrates understanding.

Providing the child with concrete apparatus would support both the assessment of the knowledge held and the development of conceptual understanding rather than the purely abstract knowledge currently demonstrated. This is the difference between knowing something and understanding it. The mastery pedagogy requires learners to develop an understanding of the relationships and connections between different ideas and the ability to apply the mathematics to new and novel situations (Askew et al., 2015; Drury, 2015). It is unlikely, although not impossible, that the 4-year-old mentioned will be able to fulfil these requirements; therefore, we need to provide interesting and challenging opportunities to develop a deeper understanding of the material.

Developing metacognition to extend learners' understanding

Metacognition is one of the five strands of the Singapore problem-solving mathematics curriculum. It is the process of being able to monitor and evaluate your own thought processes and self-regulating your learning (Quigley et al., 2018). It has been described as cognition of cognition, thinking about thinking, or – in the words of Lee (2015) – 'mind-boggling' for many teachers. However, metacognitive skills are a key part of the problem-solving process as learners need to reflect on why they chose a particular approach, rather than simply using the method provided by the teacher, monitor their thinking, and evaluate the effectiveness of the approach applied (i.e. open up the 'black box'). These processes will enable them to formulate an approach to unfamiliar problems or contexts. Teachers can facilitate this by encouraging learners to question themselves, voice their thoughts aloud or discuss with others what they are thinking. The verbalisation of mathematics using mathematical language, providing explanations and justifications, sits soundly within the English National Curriculum and has long been known as important to developing understanding: 'At all stages, pupils should be encouraged to discuss and justify the methods which they use' (Cockcroft, 1982, p458).

Are you sure?

Asking the question 'Are you sure?', particularly if asked when the learner is correct rather than using it as the more traditional response to an incorrect response, allows them to reflect on their answer, check their methods and then justify their response. It is an easy way of encouraging 'self-regulation' as when used regularly, learners will develop the habit of checking before they tell their teacher their response, often by trying an alternative method to ensure that they have reached the correct conclusion.

REFLECTIVE QUESTION

Does mastery cater to the needs of all learners?

Should we teach a mastery curriculum?

In this chapter, we have seen that a mastery curriculum takes the early ideas from Bloom (1968) and Carroll (1970) and augments these ideas with the findings of a range of educational psychologists to ensure good teaching of mathematics.

What do we mean by good teaching?

Mathematics: Understanding the Score (Ofsted, 2008) summarises the essentials of good mathematics teaching. Careful planning, although not specified, is implicit in the features of good mathematics teaching highlighted: lessons develop understanding; the teaching focuses on learning rather than doing; and lessons are part of a clear developmental sequence linked to earlier learning. Effective classroom strategies are also highlighted in the report:

- an expectation that learners provide explanations of their reasoning;

- teachers monitor understanding throughout the lesson;

- the work challenges all learners;

- non-routine problems are used by all learners;

- learners develop independence and confidence;

- teachers show good subject knowledge to make links to other learning; and

- learners 'exude enjoyment and involvement in the lesson'.

(Ofsted, 2008, pp4–5)

RESEARCH

Why are 'connectionist' teachers more successful in providing deep learning opportunities?

Effective Teachers of Numeracy (Askew et al., 1997) was a study of 90 English primary mathematics teachers that identified key factors which made some teachers more effective at teaching numeracy than others. One of the main features identified by the authors was the ability of teachers to make links across different areas of mathematics and with the real world, 'connectionist teachers', to enable learners to develop a deep and rich understanding.

Reynolds and Muijs (1999) reviewed effective teaching from America and Britain and drew some highly interesting conclusions that could now be described as a mastery approach: whole-class interactive teaching; having high expectations for learners; the use of 'small steps' for teaching all knowledge; showing how learning fits together (making connections); providing immediate help; requiring extended reasoning; discovery and problem-solving; learners taking responsibility for their own learning (self-regulated learning); and rich verbalisation of the mathematics by learners.

(Continued)

(Continued)

The findings of Ma (1999) (discussed in more detail in Chapter 5) echo those of Askew et al. (1997), who found that 'highly effective' or 'connectionist' teachers emphasised the links between the different areas of the mathematics curriculum, choosing appropriate links at the appropriate time and applying what is known to new situations. The Cockcroft Report (1982) found that 'in order to apply mathematics it was necessary not only to have mastered procedures but also to have a connected understanding of mathematical ideas and practice in solving problems' (Brown, 2014, p6).

A final point to note is made by Mason and Spence (1999, p156) regarding practice: while practice increases facility and reduces the amount of attention required, it is insufficient unless the learners' attention is also focused on what is happening in the mathematics.

Having evaluated all of the evidence in this chapter, it is difficult to see why a mastery approach should not be adopted in a classroom. Essentially, the current national focus on mastery pedagogy reinforms us of the aspects of good-quality teaching that have been established over decades.

REFLECTIVE QUESTION

What does good mathematics teaching look like?

CHAPTER SUMMARY

Key points covered in this chapter are:

* the importance of the development of conceptual understanding in facilitating learners' long-term success in mathematics;
* the fact that once something is learnt well, that learning is embedded and sustained;
* a consideration of the background of the mastery approach and why it was implemented in England;
* the provision of both support and challenge to ensure that all learners can access the mathematics at an appropriate level;
* the consistency over decades of what research has found to be good mathematics teaching.

Further reading

Bates, B. (2016) *Learning Theories Simplified*. London: SAGE.

Bob Bates has given a brief, but clear, outline of a wide range of learning theories. The book can provide a starting point for further reading or simply inform a reader of the basics.

Boyd, P. and Ash, A. (2018) 'Teachers framing exploratory learning within a textbook-based Singapore maths mastery approach'. *TEAN Journal*, 10(101): 62–73.

This paper reports research into Singapore mathematics mastery by seven teachers supported by an academic. It is highly relevant to classroom practice as it explores the use of the *Maths – No Problem!* textbook scheme to implement the mastery approach.

Lockhart, P. (2009) *A Mathematician's Lament*. New York: Bellevue Press.

Lockhart uses the metaphor of a nightmare in this book. His love of mathematics as a beautiful and creative subject and the horror of how he perceived that it was taught in schools is clear throughout the book.

Ma, L. (2010) *Knowing and Teaching Elementary Mathematics: Teachers' Understanding of Fundamental Mathematics in China and the United States*, 2nd edn. Abingdon: Routledge.

This is the anniversary edition of the original book that was based on Ma's PhD thesis. It questions why Chinese teachers with less education than their American counterparts were more confident in teaching elementary mathematics. Ma's writing is highly accessible and many of the points made in the book support current classroom practice.

References

Askew, M., Rhodes, V., Brown, M., Wiliam, D. and Johnson, D. (1997) *Effective Teachers of Numeracy*. London: King's College.

Askew, M., Bishop S., Christie C., Eaton, S., Griffin, P. and Morgan, D. (2015) *Teaching for Mastery: Questions, Tasks and Activities to Support Assessment*. Oxford: Oxford University Press.

Bloom, B.S. (1968) 'Learning for mastery'. *Evaluation Comment*, 1(2): 1–12.

Bloom, B.S. (1984) 'The search for methods of group instruction as effective as one-to-one tutoring'. *Educational Researcher*, 13(6): 4–16.

Boaler, J. (2013) 'Ability and mathematics: the mindset revolution that is reshaping education'. *Forum*, 55(1): 143–52.

Boaler, J. (2016) *Mathematical Mindsets*. San Francisco, CA: Jossey-Bass.

Boylan, M., Wolstenholme, C., Demack, S., Maxwell, B., Jay, T., Adams, G. and Reaney, S. (2019) *Longitudinal Evaluation of the Mathematics Teacher Exchange: China–England – Final Report*. London: DfE.

Brown, M. (2014) 'The Cockcroft Report: time past, time present and time future'. *Mathematics Teaching*, 243: 5–9.

Bruner, J.S. (1966) *Toward a Theory of Instruction*. Cambridge, MA: Belknap Press of Harvard University Press.

Carroll, J.B. (1970) 'Problems of measurement related to the concept of learning for mastery'. *Educational Horizons*, 48(3): 71–80.

Cockcroft, W.H. (1982) *Mathematics Counts: Report of the Committee of Inquiry into the Teaching of Mathematics in Schools in England and Wales*. London: HMSO.

Cuoco, A., Goldenberg, E.P. and Mark, J. (1996) 'Habits of mind: an organizing principle for mathematics curricula'. *Journal of Mathematical Behaviour*, 15(4): 375–402.

Department for Education (DfE) (2012) *Review of the National Curriculum in England: What Can We Learn from the English, Mathematics and Science Curricula of High-Performing Jurisdictions?* London: DfE.

Department for Education (DfE) (2013) *Key Stages 1 and 2 National Curriculum in England*. London: DfE.

Drury, H. (2015) *Mastering Mathematics*. Oxford: Oxford University Press.

Forgasz, H. and Leder, G. (2008) 'Beliefs about mathematics and mathematics teaching'. In P. Sullivan and T. Wood (eds), *The International Handbook of Mathematics Teacher Education Vol. 1*. Rotterdam: Sense, pp173–94.

Gu, L., Huang, R. and Marton, F. (2004) 'Teaching with variation: a Chinese way of promoting effective mathematics learning'. In L. Fan, N.Y. Wong, J. Cai and S. Li (eds), *How Chinese Learn Mathematics: Perspectives from Insiders*. Singapore: World Scientific Publishing, pp309–47.

Guskey, T.R. (2010) 'Lessons of mastery learning'. *Educational Leadership*, 68(2): 52–7.

Hall, J., Lindorff, A. and Sammons, P. (2016) *Evaluation of the Impact and Implementation of Inspire Maths in Year 1 Classrooms in England: Findings from a Mixed-Method Randomised Control Trial*. Oxford: Oxford University Press.

Hansen, A., Drews, D., Dudgeon, J., Lawton, F. and Surtees, L. (2017) *Children's Errors in Mathematics*, 4th edn. London: SAGE.

Hoong, Y.L., Kin, W.H. and Pien, L.C. (2015) 'Concrete–pictorial–abstract: surveying its origins and charting its future'. *The Mathematics Educator*, 16(1): 1–18.

Jerrim, J. and Vignoles, A. (2015) *The Causal Effect of East Asian 'Mastery' Teaching Methods on English Children's Mathematics Skills?* Working Paper, 15-05, London: Institute of Education.

Kilpatrick, J., Swafford, J. and Findell, B. (2001) 'The strands of mathematical proficiency'. In J. Kilpatrick and B. Findell (eds), *Adding It Up: Helping Children Learn Mathematics*. Washington, DC: National Academies Press, pp115–55.

Lee, N.H. (2015) *Metacognition in the Math Classroom*. Available at: https://singteach.nie.edu.sg/issue54-research02/

Ma, L. (1999) *Knowing and Teaching Elementary Mathematics: Teachers' Understanding of Fundamental Mathematics in China and the United States*. Mahwah, NJ: Lawrence Erlbaum.

Mason, J. and Spence, M. (1999) 'Beyond mere knowledge of mathematics: the importance of knowing to act in the moment'. *Educational Studies in Mathematics*, 383(1): 135–61.

National Association of Mathematics Advisors (NAMA) (2016) 'Five myths of mastery in mathematics'. *Mathematics Teaching*, 251: 20–4.

NCETM (2017) *Supporting Research, Evidence and Argument*. Available at: www.ncetm.org.uk/resources/50819

Ofsted (2008) *Mathematics: Understanding the Score*. London: Crown Copyright.

Oxford Encyclopedic English Dictionary (1991) Oxford: Oxford University Press.

Pozzi, S. (2013) 'Making sense of the current changes in the mathematics curriculum in England'. *Mathematics in School*, 42(3): 2–8.

Quigley, A., Muijs, D. and Stringer, E. (2018) *Metacognition and Self-Regulated Learning*. London: EEF.

Rattan, A., Good, C. and Dweck, C.S. (2012) '"It's OK – not everyone can be good at math": instructors with an entity theory comfort (and demotivate) students'. *Journal of Experimental Social Psychology*, 48(3): 731–7.

Reynolds, D. and Muijs, D. (1999) 'The effective teaching of mathematics: a review of research'. *School Leadership and Management*, 19(3): 273–88.

Rycroft-Smith, L. and Boylan, M. (2019) 'Mastery in mathematics'. *Espresso*. Available at: www.cambridgemaths.org/Images/espresso_16_mastery_in_mathematics.pdf

Stripp, C. (2014) *Mastery in Mathematics: What It Is and Why We Should Be Doing It*. Available at: www.ncetm.org.uk/resources/45776

Trundley, R., Wreghitt, C., Edginton, H., Eversett, H. and Burke, S. (2017) *Supporting Children to Be Active and Influential Participants in Mathematics Lessons through Effective Use of Assigning Competence and Pre-Teaching*. Available at: www.babcock-education.co.uk/ldp/primarymaths

Vygotsky, L.S. (2011) 'The dynamics of the schoolchild's mental development in relation to teaching and learning'. *Journal of Cognitive Education and Psychology*, 10(2): 198–211.

3

COORDINATION OF MATHEMATICS IN A MASTERY ENVIRONMENT

PINKY JAIN AND ROSALYN HYDE

KEYWORDS: CONSISTENCY; PROGRESSION; COLLABORATIVE PLANNING; ASSESSMENT; INTERVENTION

CHAPTER OBJECTIVES

This chapter will allow you to achieve the following outcomes:

- develop an understanding of the challenges related to the management of mathematics learning for mastery across the school;
- appreciate the key features that might need further consideration in your school in order to establish a mastery approach to teaching mathematics;
- understand the need to appreciate the embedding of a mastery approach across your school.

Introduction

The most frequently mentioned enabling factors … were staff responsiveness, resources, senior leadership commitment, and implementation leadership.

(Boylan et al., 2019, p128)

In this chapter, we will explore some of the questions that using a mastery approach raises for mathematics coordinators and heads of mathematics. For example, is it possible for only part of a primary school or secondary school mathematics department to take on a mastery approach to teaching mathematics? In the Shanghai model of mastery, the teacher research group is an essential part of teacher life; to what extent is this replicable in an English context, and on what scale? By the end of this chapter, you should have a better understanding of some of the issues raised by leaders of mathematics in schools, such as managing progression, assessment and consistency throughout schools, as well as considering if consistency is really needed, and to some extent what it looks like, what the key considerations are, and whether these are achievable. The chapter also considers some ways of supporting staff development and enhancing their skills to meet the needs of a mastery approach. We will consider a range of approaches that you could tailor for your school and the teams you are working with. Even if you are not leading mathematics in your school, this chapter will give you an insight as to how all the directions you are given by your mathematics lead connect together as a wider frame of reference for your teaching.

This chapter covers both primary and secondary leadership of mathematics. There are many common challenges and common solutions that are shared within this chapter. However, where there are distinct differences between secondary and primary, these are highlighted in the chapter and linked to relevant Key Stages for ease of understanding.

RESEARCH

The evidence for the efficacy of mastery practices

Boylan et al.'s (2018) paper considers a range of pedagogical approaches they consider to be components of English approaches to mastery and the existing research evidence of their impact on learner outcomes. These approaches were identified through their evaluation of the mathematics teacher exchange programme that took place in 2014. As they point out, many of the classroom practices advocated by mastery approaches are considered to be good practice in any case. The study summarises their findings by suggesting there is evidence that the following practices impact on attainment and should be considered as priorities for implementation in the primary classroom:

- interactive dialogue and mathematical problems/tasks that promote this;
- a greater use of models and representations, with multiple models used in relation to the same mathematical concepts; and
- responsive teaching using formative assessment.

(Boylan et al., 2018, pp22-3)

They further recommend that 'mathematically focused, embedded and close to practice collaborative professional development' (Boylan et al., 2018, p24) is needed in order to change teachers' practice.

(Continued)

(Continued)

However, they also identify a number of practices that they say require further research evaluation in order to evidence their impact on attainment. The features of mastery this applies to are:

- whole-class mastery teaching;
- use of textbooks (and specifically those recommended to schools);
- curriculum pace;
- memorising factual knowledge;
- precise use of language; and
- mastery-focused CPD.

(Boylan et al., 2018, p24)

Managing mathematics learning

All leaders and their teams aim to establish teaching throughout their school which ensures that children are able to develop a deep understanding of mathematics and to progress developmentally from year to year. Other than the internal desire of teachers to ensure good management of learning, there are external factors that also come into play when considering the implementation of a mastery approach throughout the school. While there is no specific mention of 'mastery' in it, the current National Curriculum (DfE, 2014) has clear aims to ensure that all pupils gain fluency in mathematics, are able to reason mathematically, and can solve problems. Such aims incorporate the deep understanding at the root of mastery approaches to mathematics, and the National Curriculum is the dominant document for planning what is taught in schools. It explains 'how mathematics is an interconnected subject in which pupils need to be able to move fluently between representations of mathematical ideas' (Mooney et al., 2014, p4).

At both the primary and secondary level, the slower curriculum coverage advocated by a mastery approach is only possible when there is a whole-school commitment through strategic development to approaching teaching of mathematics. The challenges that teachers face are that 'teaching can be seen as taking place in time, while learning takes place over time' (Griffin, 1989, p12). The content-driven demand of the curriculum has meant that mathematics has often been taught, and has been perceived as having been taught, in a disconnected way, in small chunks of content from the curriculum. For example, you may see lessons in primary schools where addition is being taught in isolation and then a separate lesson on subtraction, with little connectivity between the two concepts.

As identified in Chapter 1, the dominant model of curriculum design in secondary mathematics has been that of the spiral curriculum attributed to Bruner (GTCE, 2006), typically enacted as two-week blocks of teaching for each mathematical topic, with the topic revisited and developed in later years. The experience of learners with this curriculum model is sometimes more akin to repeating the same material rather than developing understanding. As GCSE examinations approach in Key Stage 4, the nature of our high-stakes examination system in England means that teachers often feel under pressure to cover as much of the curriculum content as quickly as possible, sacrificing depth of understanding in the hopes of gaining 'quick fixes' for examination marks. However, connections need to be made between the concepts of mathematics throughout lessons in order to meet the aims set out by the National Curriculum programme of study (DfE, 2014). Therefore, how can subject leads and teachers of mathematics manage this progression and ensure connectedness?

The vast majority of primary school teachers train as generalist teachers and do not hold mathematics qualifications at post-GCSE level. In secondary schools, teachers are, of course, trained as subject specialists, but the well-documented shortage of mathematics teachers in England means that many of those teaching mathematics in secondary schools are non-specialists. For the mathematics lead in a secondary school, consideration as to how to deploy specialists is important. Often non-specialists are allocated to the 'bottom sets' in lower years. However, in our experience, these are the classes that need most specialist support, given that some students may have long-standing complex difficulties with mathematics and/or other difficulties to manage. Teaching high-attaining classes at lower secondary level might provide non-specialists with good opportunities to develop their subject knowledge and expertise as a mathematics teacher. Planning for development of non-specialists over a period of several years can also encourage them to be more committed to teaching mathematics, feel part of the mathematics team, and be more invested in their own learning journey towards specialism. The importance of subject knowledge and ways of developing it are discussed in detail in Chapter 5.

For primary teachers and even more so primary mathematics leads, there are three key tools that can be used to support this demand: the programmes of study, mapping of small steps, and working collaboratively. This third tool is discussed much later in the chapter. The *programme of study*, which dictates the content that needs to be taught, can be used as a firm starting point. This states that content must be covered in two-year blocks as assessment takes place at the end of each two-year block. So, within Year 1 and 2, all that is stated in the programme of study needs to be covered by the end of Year 2, and for Year 3 and 4 by the end of Year 4, and so on. This allows for the possibility of moving away from considering the content in a linear manner and in one-year blocks, and allows greater flexibility of how content can be sequenced throughout the two years. For example, in Shanghai, children spend a large amount of their time at the ages of 5 and 6 covering the four operations and number, spending an average of 146 hours on number as compared to an average of 22 hours on graphics and geometry (Isaacs et al., 2015). This gives some indication of a possible way forward, as having good number sense and a connected understanding of number is the key to ensuring future development in mathematics. So, a key question in the management of progression is to consider the balance of time given to each area of mathematics and where emphasis is placed. Mathematics leads have an opportunity to consider strategically the degree of time and emphasis given to different aspects of mathematics, and not merely to follow the order stated in the programme of study. That such an approach is possible is indicated in Boylan et al.'s (2017) report of their longitudinal study of the China–England teacher exchange programme. Approximately one-third of the primary schools in the study had changed their school timetable in order to support implementation of a Shanghai teaching-style model for mathematics lessons. However, schools were more likely to make changes to classroom practices rather than structural whole-school change.

Teachers need to consider the delivery of each element of content and whether, for example, spending Year 1 covering only number, place value and the four operations, and then in Year 2 covering other areas of mathematics from the Year 1 and 2 programme of study, would allow for a deeper and more meaningful understanding to be developed. A second tool for defining and managing progression is the *mapping of small steps* to develop and embed understanding. In primary schools in

England, progression has traditionally been seen as moving from one year to the next and covering the content for each year, with each new teacher starting from their own starting point. This causes a few problems, one of which being how teachers make the connections needed and the other being a lack of consistency in what is being covered. Unfortunately, school schemes of work are sometimes limited to identifying 'slices of knowledge' that are presented arbitrarily as, for example, autumn term blocks of knowledge, covering place value, addition and subtraction, shape and data, money, and then time. What would be of great benefit to support and develop deep conceptual understanding is the mapping of the small steps needed to embed understanding of each concept. The case study considers one possible approach.

CASE STUDY

Curriculum design

This approach to curriculum design was used by a small number of primary schools who have carried out the following steps to achieve a more ergonomic way of planning and embedding the mastery approach.

1. Identify key concepts in mathematics that are within the programme of study (note, this is not the same as content; fractions is content, but a key concept within this is understanding parts of a whole).

2. Map collaboratively all the steps needed for children to ensure that they have mastered that concept. In order to achieve this, schools found it easier to start with Year 6 and consider the concepts needed to achieve the outcomes in Year 6, working back through the steps needed to be at that level of understanding. For example, with addition, what does a child who truly understands the concept of addition need to know from the first step of being able to count, to understanding the commutative nature of addition? Initially, these steps are laid out without consideration of year groups, but just as ideas. Doing this mapping allows for the interconnectedness that is key to mastering mathematics to be realised. The trick (and challenge) is to spend time in making the steps small enough to ensure that there is no omission in the building blocks needed to develop deep understanding of each mathematical concept.

3. The next step is to add vocabulary, models and images, and key indications of what the child will be able to do at each stage. Again, this is considered using a whole-school approach.

4. The last stage is the sectioning of the steps into which year groups they will take place in and what the lessons need to cover in terms of outcomes from children's learning.

The advantages of this approach are that it requires the whole school to be involved and to develop collaboratively an understanding of what comes before and after the particular year group individuals might be teaching in, which is the third key tool. Also, it allows for a clear direction to be given as to where learning is headed. There are some difficulties with this approach experienced by some schools, such as the time it takes to achieve this level of detail, the strong subject knowledge required of all teachers and the need for all staff to work in this way. However, with resources being available to start the process, such as the NCETM (2014) progression maps, it is possible to start with a populated template and work as a whole school to achieve this level of progression-mapping.

Taking the time collaboratively to develop such a level of detail in the concepts being covered increases the vested interests in ensuring that there is common understanding and a community of practice between colleagues. This ensures that the management of learning is developed in a way that allows teachers to have autonomy and use judgement when teaching, which is based on a deeper knowledge of mathematics.

REFLECTIVE QUESTIONS

In what ways is mathematics managed in your school or department to support a mastery approach? What are the challenges to current practice?

Consistency in approach

Leong et al. (2015) state that the concrete–pictorial–abstract approach (see Chapter 5) is a key approach to teaching mathematics in Singapore and is widely used. We might therefore hypothesise that the widely reported success of their mathematics teaching is at least partly a consequence of consistency in approach. Hence, we will examine what it means to be consistent in teaching. One of the values underpinning the English education system is that while the National Curriculum defines the general approach and content for mathematics, schools have a degree of autonomy as to how they enact this. This means that some schools have developed distinctly different approaches to teaching and learning mathematics compared with others. Can we really, or should we, have the same approach to teaching mathematics across all schools? This is a perplexing question in that it is irrelevant whether the answer is to be consistent or not to be consistent, as they are both wrong. If we suggest yes, then we should all have the same approach as this will ensure that all children get the same input and there are no omissions in teaching. We come up against knowing that all children are different and may not succeed with one approach, and that teachers are different and may not be at the same level of skills. On the other hand, if we allow for all teachers to teach in a manner they choose, then there is a danger of confusion for both teachers and children as they go through the school system. Making the question of consistency binary ensures that we make an unsatisfactory choice. How can it then be possible in the classroom to act consistently?

Understanding how consistency can be achieved requires a definition of consistency and what it might look like. There is a mistaken view that to be consistent in our teaching, we have to do the same things. For example, in many schools and academy chains (groups of schools), mathematics teaching is organised using common schemes of work with shared resources and an expectation that teachers will all use the same materials at the same time. Does this make things consistent? Yes, it does. However, does it ensure that deep learning takes place? We would hazard a guess and state no as there is very little scope for teacher judgement or autonomy. Also, there is no recognition of the learner as being an individual with different starting points and, as Akbar (2018) suggests, 'The endeavour to get everyone teaching in the same way risks crippling two of the most important traits of any good teacher: their personality and their ability to build relationships'. It is also the case that in Shanghai, while content is defined on a lesson-by-lesson basis, teachers use their professional judgement to make pedagogical decisions.

What we need to state is the purpose for which we are holding the ideal of consistency so strongly. What is needed is not robotic autonomous consistency, but for schools to decide the principles that need to be consistent and then allow teachers to develop individual ways to achieve these. For example, use of the concrete–pictorial–abstract approach is only effective if there is agreement between all teachers about what concrete resources will be used to explore different areas of mathematics. If, for example, one teacher chooses to use Dienes cubes and another in the following year uses place value counters, this is fine if links are made between these two manipulatives. However, if one manipulative is discarded and a new manipulative is used without any links to previous manipulatives, then there is an element of relearning that has to take place and the children have to go through cognitive translation to be able to use the new model to build on their understanding. Therefore, what is really valuable is to consider the key elements that need to be consistent in each lesson and throughout the school. The following case study exemplifies one approach to developing consistency at primary school level.

CASE STUDY

The 'perfect six'

The primary mathematics team at the University of Worcester have developed a model for teachers establishing key principles that need to be consistent to have maximum impact on learning, which they call the 'perfect six'. Figure 3.1 shows the key elements of what research has identified must be included to have the greatest impact on conceptual understanding.

How does this work in school and your teaching? The primary mathematics team recommend that when planning lessons, you consider how you can include opportunities for the following:

- The talk and range of language used. Planning for the vocabulary to be used, as stated earlier, needs to be decided across the whole school to ensure that there is common understanding.
- What are the models and images that can support children to understand the concepts that you are working on? Are there key concrete resources that would support conceptual understanding? Think about this across all year groups.
- What are the connections that you can make in the lessons to areas children already know and other areas of mathematics that your topic can be connected to, ensuring that you are not teaching topics in isolation? The whole planning model discussed earlier, which breaks concepts down into small steps, supports this.
- Consider at the planning stage the key questions that need to be asked to embed learning, and more so understanding. These are not just closed questions about the mathematics, but about supporting reasoning.
- Ensure children have opportunities to solve problems and enable reasoning as this will ensure that children deepen understanding not just at the end, but throughout the learning experience.
- Misconceptions should be part of every lesson. Think about the possible misconceptions that might be linked to the concepts you are working on. Share them with the class and use them as a learning opportunity.

To summarise, therefore, in order to achieve consistency, what is essentially required is that as a whole school, there is common agreement of the six areas suggested by the 'perfect six', and that they will be part of all teaching.

Concrete–pictorial–abstract (CPA approach)

The three steps (or representations) are used so that **all** children of **all** ages develop conceptual understanding. A 'hands-on, minds-on' approach, involving:

Concrete – manipulatives/objects to handle

Pictorial – drawings, diagrams and images

Abstract – mathematical notation

Making connections

Opportunities for pupils to:

- try a range of ways to carry out their work and make connections to a range of mathematical concepts;
- see examples of mathematical concepts and how they link.

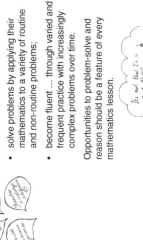

Language and talk

Mathematical vocabulary is used accurately by both the teacher and the children. Mathematics lessons have a focus on talk and discussion.

Subject Knowledge

Mathematics Perfect Six

Supporting Mastery

Misconceptions

Misconceptions are planned for, exposed and openly discussed.

Problem-solving and reasoning

The aims of the mathematics National Curriculum are for all pupils to:

- reason mathematically;
- solve problems by applying their mathematics to a variety of routine and non-routine problems;
- become fluent ... through varied and frequent practice with increasingly complex problems over time.

Opportunities to problem-solve and reason should be a feature of every mathematics lesson.

Questioning

Open questions are asked that stimulate mathematical thinking and discussion:

- Can you explain your thinking?
- Is there another way?
- Why did you ...?

Children are encouraged to ask their own questions to help clarify their understanding.

UoW_2019 ©

Figure 3.1   The 'perfect six'

It is possible that as a school, you may develop your own version of key principles that you feel will support the embedding of mastery. However, the fact remains that there needs to be common agreement across schools in order to embed a mastery approach to teaching. How this might evolve will be left up to teachers to use their skills and knowledge of the children they are teaching. So, lessons may not look the same, but the principles should run through the whole school, like letters in a stick of rock that will support the management of mastery learning for each child.

At the secondary level, there is also a need for a consistent approach. In many secondary schools, there is a degree of autonomy between teachers as to how they cover the yearly curriculum content and what resources they use. This potentially leads to teachers approaching mathematics lessons from different theoretical and practical standpoints. Classes following a mastery approach will be covering the curriculum content apparently more slowly in order that the mathematics learning is developed more securely and in greater depth. Therefore, in schools where whole year groups sit regular common assessments, those classes following a mastery approach may appear to achieve less well because they have covered less curriculum content, and therefore have not yet studied some of the content of the assessment. In many secondary schools, teaching for mastery approaches are used within an environment where learners are grouped by attainment, which makes moving between groups difficult if some teachers use mastery approaches and others do not. Progression from one year to the next also becomes difficult for learners if they move between teachers taking fundamentally different approaches to teaching mathematics.

Developing an approach that is both consistent and flexible is not easy, and Boylan et al. (2017) identify striking the balance between flexibility of implementation and consistency as an issue for schools taking up mastery. Davis and Sumara (2006) helpfully sum up the approach as follows:

Building a successful community means recognising and using the mathematical strengths learners bring to the classroom, not looking at what they cannot do and trying to fill gaps. Looking at classrooms through the lens of complexity theory indicates that diversity is actually a key catalyst in the emergence of ideas.

(p86)

REFLECTIVE QUESTIONS

What models and representations (see also Chapter 5) are used in your school? Are they used consistently? Are links made between them where teachers make different choices?

Meeting the needs of individual learners

Having addressed the management of learning, what it means to be consistent and establishing a working definition of consistency, we need to consider some of the common features in schools that support learning. Note that the aim is not to have a detailed debate on these areas, as they deserve a book in their own right, but to consider the form these might take when developing a whole-school approach to mastery, as well as some of the challenges. Other chapters have considered some of these ideas too, but the intention here is about how to enable choices to be made in relation to strategically deciding whether intervention is even the best way forward.

In secondary schools, and often at upper primary age, it is common to group learners according to prior attainment. In secondary schools in particular, setting policies can limit opportunities for learners and, in our opinion, can become a self-fulfilling prophecy in that low-attaining learners may perform down to the expectations their teachers have of them. That having been said, the range of attainment in a typical comprehensive school means that some flexible and limited grouping by attainment may be helpful to support teachers in meeting the needs of both low and high attainers. However, as discussed in Chapter 1, a mastery approach supports the view that all learners can understand mathematics if they are given sufficient time and support to do so.

One strategy for supporting learners, particularly in primary schools, is the use of interventions. Intervention is often used as a deficit model and offered to a child or children at risk of falling behind. Mathematics leads need to consider whether in their school these are the only groups who might benefit from extra support. Therefore, the definition of intervention needs to be extended from children with poor attainment to any children who need extra support.

There is limited research on the effectiveness of mathematics intervention in schools. The challenge that Wilson and Räsänen (2008) suggest is:

> *Many studies fail to meet most of the requirements for high quality intervention studies, which is a reflection of the high monetary cost of and practical difficulties associated with such research. In particular, single-case publications and studies with very small numbers of participants are common, despite the fact that they limit generalization.*

(p1)

This means that there are no clear reviewed approaches that work better than others to support the selection of effective interventions. This is not necessarily detrimental as it allows for a range of tools to be available that need to be tried and tested by your settings to support the needs of your children. Ofsted (2009), in research they carried out on interventions, also concluded that there was no one effective intervention programme. Therefore, selection needs to be managed in school to fit the needs of children. Further work carried out by Bernie and Lall (2009) concluded that when there is a whole-school approach to intervention, it is more likely to be successful. Ofsted also concluded that when teaching assistants (TAs), as is often the case in primary schools, carry out interventions, these are only effective when the TA has strong subject knowledge and there is a strong steer from the teacher. So, in order to manage interventions, though there is not one strong approach that can be applied to any school, the principles are consistent in that having a clear identification of children in need of additional support, be it for weaker students or students who need to be challenged more, is the starting point. Mathematics leads need to consider who is best placed to deliver this intervention and whether or not it should be the TA who carries it out. If TAs are to be used, then mathematics leads need to consider whether they should be part of all the planning and mapping processes in order to be able to support learning in a connected manner. The final step is to consider the nature of intervention. Different forms of interventions fall into two broad groups, in class and outside of class. The former generally consists of the TA revisiting an area that needs more support, presenting ideas that may link to future work, supporting during lessons with additional time for particular groups of children, or grouping children depending on the area of need. Outside of class support generally refers to removing small groups of children who have similar challenges, targeting individuals and supporting them outside the classroom environment. Note that support provided outside of the class often leads to widening the knowledge gap for many children. The following factors need to be considered when deciding the best intervention approach:

- clear identification of children who need support;

- careful planning of the intervention programme to meet their needs;

- subject knowledge training for all staff on how to direct intervention;

- monitoring and evaluating the impact;

- selecting the right staff to carry out intervention; and

- considering when is the best time to implement the intervention and the impact of this on children – should it be before teaching (pre-teaching) of a particular topic, during or after?

The role of the mathematics coordinator or department lead needs to include:

- strategic planning based on data analysis and resources committed to all intervention programmes;

- training and time given for the programme to realise benefits; and

- evaluating impact and ensuring that all sessions have some impact on children's understanding.

The EEF report (Sharples et al., 2018) provides further evidence regarding the complexity in making best use of TAs and provides additional advice on making effective use of additional learning support in schools.

As we have seen in other chapters, other countries have a very different view on interventions and how they cater for children of varying needs. It is false to assume that other jurisdictions do not have any form of intervention or resources invested in ensuring that the gaps between children's attainment is as narrow as possible. The difference may be that there is no overt withdrawal of children and that there is embedded intervention. For example, in Shanghai, children who struggle in a particular lesson are grouped together immediately and taught to overcome the challenges that they face on that one particular lesson so that they are able to keep up with their peers. Also, the use of rich task strategy, which allows children to access mathematics at different levels, seems to dominate as a form of intervention.

Of course, supporting the needs of individual learners also includes making provision for the highest-attaining. Previous models that schools have used have included acceleration, where those who are deemed to be 'able' or 'gifted' are given different material on topics that are considered more advanced. The difficulties with such models are that the gap between the highest- and lowest-attaining is further widened, and it can mean that the highest-attaining become isolated. It can also be difficult for teachers to manage. As identified in Chapter 1, mastery approaches promote the idea that everyone can make progress and achieve and support a model where groups of learners work on the same idea in their mathematics lessons, with the range of attainment catered for through the provision of appropriate support and challenge. Examples of these sorts of approaches can be seen in Chapters 7 and 8.

REFLECTIVE QUESTIONS

What views do you hold regarding supporting and challenging learners? What works best with your learners?

Assessment

An additional area of departmental management which is often a challenge is that of assessment. With the withdrawal of central government guidance on assessment, there has been a mixed economy throughout schools, with primary coordinators trying to consider a range of purposes for assessments that they want to implement. The key difficulty with the introduction of mastery as a concept is defining what it means to master. Is there a definitive end point that can be assessed? To have mastered something would imply that there is completion in the understanding of knowledge which is considered to be finite. Furthermore, labelling learners as emerging, secure, developing and mastering is not appropriate and does not offer what is really needed or valuable from assessment. We want assessment to shed light on where individuals are in their understanding so that as teachers we can build on this learning and develop it further. Though the external sharing of assessment data is something that is ingrained in our education system, we could argue that this has little bearing on what is of greater importance – ensuring that children make progress in every lesson and over time. Therefore, the summative assessment approaches (such as SATs, tests and exams) are not an area of focus here as they do not offer any support for developing deep understanding. The focus needs to be on ongoing formative assessment, or as Askew (2012) states:

> Children's learning in its own right is not valued; it simply is a means of checking out whether the prescribed curriculum has been correctly delivered. Formative assessment, assessment that helps teachers know what children have learnt as well as where they need support is less important than summative assessment to check off objectives. We need to be alert not to fall into confusing the map (intended curriculum) for the terrain (children's learning).

(p23)

In order to embed the mastery approach, we need to consider movement away from tests and end point assessments as they are a crude tool to establish knowledge that may or may not have been acquired, and they come too late in the learning process to have any impact as time has already passed and learning opportunities have been missed. Davis (1996) uses the terms from 'preformed to performed', and Askew (2012) explains that the move is 'from knowledge – the predetermined, pre-formed collection of mathematical "bits" to knowing – the performing of being mathematical' (p25).

It is this notion of 'being mathematical' that encapsulates mastery at all levels, and assessments should be designed to assess the degree to which children are being mathematical and how to move them in the correct direction. In terms of the role of mathematics leads, this requires a level of braveness to support teams to worry less about summative assessment and more about formative assessment strategies. Ofsted's (2011) report on mathematical understanding explores these ideas, and suggests that 'for a variety of reasons, teachers find it easier to assess pupils' knowledge and skills rather than their understanding' (p48). They go on to suggest that this is often related to teachers' own subject knowledge and skills. Therefore, mathematics leads need to ensure that all teachers have strong subject knowledge and have support to develop their questioning skills, as it is the way in which we ask questions while children are carrying out their work that will deepen understanding and enhance mastery (see Chapter 5). The key feature of any assessment should be that it is querying understanding, not skills and knowledge, and that it offers information that will support the learner in future endeavours. It is always helpful in such situations to work together and develop a framework that allows formative assessment in different structures.

Working collaboratively

In this section, we return to the third tool. So far, the strongest themes emerging from the discussions in relation to embedding and managing conceptual understanding in a mastery approach are that of the need for consistency and for working collaboratively as a team. Hairon and Tan (2017) say 'there is a broad international consensus' that professional learning communities are groups 'of people sharing and critically interrogating their practice in an ongoing, reflective, collaborative, inclusive, learning-oriented, and growth-promoting way' (p92). One of the notable features of mathematics teaching in both Shanghai and Singapore is that considerable time and attention is devoted to professional development, and collaborative professional development in particular. In Shanghai, much of this takes the format of teacher research groups, where a lesson is taught by one teacher and observed by several others. Following the lesson, time is spent discussing the lesson, focusing on how the lesson might be improved and developed to enhance the outcomes for learners. This is in contrast to the English approach to lesson observation, which tends to focus on making a quality judgement of some kind, rather than on a supportive approach seeking to develop teaching to improve learning.

We believe non-judgemental shared planning, observation and focused discussion all to be powerful tools in continuing professional development for teachers, whatever stage they are in their career. Chapter 7 provides detailed case studies of both a teacher research group in practice and of the Japanese lesson study approach and their impacts on teacher practice. Both these case studies exemplify Boylan et al.'s (2018) recommendation that effective professional development needs to focus on mathematics, be close to practice and be collaborative. These case studies also provide models that can include beginning teachers, student teachers and teaching assistants. Chapter 5 identifies that having excellent subject knowledge is vital to teaching for conceptual understanding and further suggests that collaborative working is a good way of developing teacher subject knowledge.

CHAPTER SUMMARY

Key points covered in this chapter are:

- a range of factors that are important in coordinating a mastery approach across a school or department;
- some of the challenges facing those who are mathematics leads in their setting;
- the importance of understanding what we mean by consistency and how that might be implemented across a school or department;
- the value of collaborative approaches to teacher development.

Further reading

Drury, H. (2018) *Mastering Mathematics: Teaching to Transform Achievement*. Oxford: Oxford University Press.

Drury, H. (2018) *How to Teach Mathematics for Mastery*. Oxford: Oxford University Press.

Both of Helen Drury's books provide useful insights across the issues raised in this chapter.

References

Akbar, O. (2018) 'Why whole-school consistency is overrated'. *Times Education Supplement*, 4 July.

Askew, M. (2012) *Transforming Primary Mathematics*. Abingdon: Routledge.

Bernie, J. and Lall, M. (2008) *Building Bridges between Home and School Mathematics: A Review of the Ocean Mathematics Project*. London: UCL Institute of Education.

Boylan, M., Maxwell, B., Wolstenholme, C. and Jay, T. (2017) *Longitudinal Evaluation of the Mathematics Teacher Exchange: China–England – Third Interim Report*. London: DfE.

Boylan, M., Maxwell, B., Wolstenholme, C., Jay, T. and Demack, S. (2018) 'The mathematics teacher exchange and "mastery" in England: the evidence for the efficacy of component practices'. *Education Sciences*, 8(4): 202.

Boylan, M., Wolstenholme, C., Demack, S., Maxwell, B., Jay, T., Adams, G. and Reaney, S. (2019) *Longitudinal Evaluation of the Mathematics Teacher Exchange: China–England – Final Report*. London: DfE.

Davis, B. (1996) *Teaching Mathematics: Toward a Sound Alternative*. London: Routledge.

Davis, B. and Sumara, D. (2006) *Complexity and Education: Inquiries into Learning, Teaching and Research*. London: Lawrence Erlbaum Associates.

Department for Education (DfE) (2014) *The National Curriculum in England: Complete Framework for Key Stages 1 to 4*. Available at: www.gov.uk/government/publications/national-curriculum-in-england-framework-for-key-stages-1-to-4

General Teaching Council for England (GTCE) (2006) *Jerome Bruner's Constructivist Model and the Spiral Curriculum for Teaching and Learning*. Available at: http://curee.co.uk/node/4849

Griffin, P. (1989) 'Teaching takes place in time, learning takes place over time'. *Mathematics Teaching,* 126: 12–13.

Hairon, S. and Tan, C. (2017) 'Education policy borrowing in China: has the West wind overpowered the East wind?' *Compare: A Journal of Comparative and International Education,* 47(1): 91–104.

Isaacs, T., Creese, B. and Gonzalez, A. (2015) *Aligned Instructional Systems: Shanghai.* London: UCL Institute of Education.

Leong, Y.H., Ho, W.K. and Cheng, L.P. (2015) 'Concrete–pictorial–abstract: surveying its origins and charting its future'. *The Mathematics Educator,* 16(1): 1–18.

Mooney, C., Hansen, A., Ferrie, L., Fox, S. and Wrathmell, R. (2014) *Primary Mathematics: Knowledge and Understanding,* 7th edn. London: SAGE.

NCETM (2014) *Progression Maps for Key Stages 1 and 2.* Available at: www.ncetm.org.uk/resources/42990

Ofsted (2009) *An Evaluation of National Strategy Intervention Programmes.* London: Ofsted.

Ofsted (2011) *Mathematics: Understanding the Score.* London: Ofsted.

Sharples, J., Webster, R. and Blatchford, P. (2018) *Making Best Use of Teaching Assistants: Guidance Report.* London: Education Endowment Fund.

Wilson, A.J. and Räsänen, P. (2008) 'Effective interventions for numeracy difficulties/disorders'. In *Encyclopedia of Language and Literacy Development.* London, ON: Canadian Language and Literacy Research Network, pp1–11.

4

LEARNING TO MASTER MATHEMATICS IN THE EARLY YEARS

TOM WEAVER

KEYWORDS: EARLY MATHEMATICS; SHALLOW AND DEEP LEARNING IN MATHEMATICS; PHILOSOPHY OF EARLY MATHEMATICS; MATHEMATICS AS METAPHOR; LEARNING DISPOSITIONS

CHAPTER OBJECTIVES

This chapter will allow you to achieve the following outcomes:

- reflect on your understanding of the nature of mathematics subject content in early years mathematics and its relation to mastery;

- consider the approaches to supporting children's positive mastery dispositions in mathematics;

- reflect on a range of pedagogical approaches that encourage positive dispositions in early years mathematics.

Introduction

The portrait of mathematics has a human face.

(Lakoff and Nunez, 2000, p377)

Can children in the early years master mathematical concepts? Is it possible for young children to attain a level of understanding that could be called 'mastery'? Mathematics in the early years plays a different role to that in the later years, where the focus is on mastery of subject content and the application of skills in a wide range of contexts. As it is children's initiation into the culture of mathematics learning, in the early years it is important to focus on the development of positive dispositions that *lay the foundations for later mastery of mathematics*. As such, I will be arguing that the classical approach to mathematics, which views mathematics schooling as 'involving the idealisation and simplification of a situation in order that it can be mathematised, and thus broken from its "non-mathematical" referents' (Noss and Hoyles, 1996, p3), is less suitable for learning in the early years, although it can be used effectively with older children. Instead, we will look at ways in which teachers and practitioners can approach early mathematics as a subject created by the collective human imagination (Lakoff and Nunez, 2000, p377). In this view, mathematical knowledge is embodied by neural connections that are unique to every human. Although mathematical concepts are so well constructed that they have stability over time, the context in which every learning activity takes places is unique, and so mathematics learning is never complete, but a perpetually evolving body of knowledge both for the child and for mathematics as a subject in general.

In this chapter, we will be looking specifically at the *dispositions* that support the development of positive, helpful attitudes to young children's mathematics learning in order to provide the conditions of mastery of the subject content that will, in most cases, occur during the later years of their education. By disposition we mean the cognitive, psychological, physical and emotional states that frame activity in a given area. So, rather than decontextualising and abstracting meaning, in the early years we should be contextualising meaning and grounding it in concrete experience. The chapter is divided into three sections, beginning with your disposition as a mathematics practitioner or teacher, moving on to considering the children's dispositions as they learn, and finishing with some suggestions about how pedagogy can support children's positive mastery dispositions in mathematics learning.

⎯ REFLECTIVE QUESTIONS ⎯

You want children to learn about mathematical concepts, but should you teach at a fast pace to establish understanding as quickly as possible or should you aim for more depth of understanding before moving on to more complex concepts? Can fluency and mastery of early mathematical concepts be quickly established? What are the challenges facing children's early understanding of mathematical concepts?

Your disposition: the issue of breadth or depth

A popular pedagogical approach to effective teaching is provided by the various systematic synthetic phonics schemes. In the context of early reading, the sooner the phonemes and graphemes are learnt, the sooner fluency in decoding is acquired. As there are a set number of graphemes and frequently used phonemes, phonics schemes generally encourage a fast-paced approach to learning, with helpful mnemonics and other pedagogical tools to quickly consolidate the knowledge. This type of learning can be relatively 'shallow' as once the 'rules' are established they change infrequently. Early mastery of reading also has the advantage that phonemes can be related to maps of meaning which already exist in spoken language, and so for most children there is already an established pattern of oral language use to which the phonemes and graphemes can be applied. In general, the acquisition of early reading skills is regarded as time-limited as it is very unlikely that fluent readers will revisit the *concept* of individual phonemes once they have been learnt, although the basic skills are *applied* throughout a reader's life as they encounter new words.

So what about early mathematics skills? Are these similar in nature to early phonics skills? On first appearances, they may seem to be. Children begin to learn to count, make simple addition and subtraction calculations, learn the names of shapes, and so on. Indeed, the evidence suggests that some of the very basic mathematics skills are innate (present at birth), such as subitising (recognising total amounts in small groups of numbers) and recognising small additions or subtractions to groups of objects. If we treat these concepts as the basic building blocks of mathematics understanding, then it stands to reason that – like the approach to teaching systematic synthetic phonics – we should try to help children acquire them in as short a time as possible in order for children to move on to more complex and abstract concepts. The commonest pedagogical approach to this is to see the teaching of mathematics as a process of inducting children into decontextualised forms of mathematical knowledge (Noss and Hoyles, 1996). In this view, we start with concrete examples to which pictorial and abstract concepts are applied. As soon as possible, the links to concrete examples are removed once these basic links to 'real life' are mastered. In a similar manner to acquiring phonetic understanding, once the concept of 'three' is understood in concrete terms, children can then move on to the more abstract process of applying 'the threeness of three' to problems. In this sense, early mastery of mathematics involves the ability to see the logical 'bones' of a mathematical problem that can be learnt and transferred and applied to other areas of mathematics learning. Lakatos (1976) identifies this as an idealist view of mathematics where the subject content of mathematics is seen as a set of eternal and unchangeable truths that are 'out there' waiting to be discovered. When we work with young children using this approach, we typically rely on the modelling of concepts with regular checks to see if children have understood the learning, with a strong emphasis on what is a right and a wrong answer. In a sense, we are checking that the children have 'seen' the same mathematical truth that we have.

RESEARCH

The psychology of mathematics as a subject

As practitioners and teachers, our disposition or approach to teaching a subject can be influenced by a number of factors. One of these is the psychology of the subject content, or the way we view the materials we are teaching. Getzels and Thelen (1972) studied the psychology of a range of curriculum subjects and classified them in terms of how much agency or self-direction the subject allowed the learner to have. They give an example of learning spellings as being low in learner

(Continued)

(Continued)

agency because the content of the learning is precisely given - learners get the spellings wrong if they choose their own approach to spelling words, and so must commit to learning the content by rote. At the opposite end of the scale, they give the example of art. In this subject, learners are expected to produce their own content and express their own understanding of the subject. If the learner were to trace the teacher's drawing, their work would be deemed to have limited value. These are two extremes on a continuum of curriculum subjects. Where do you think mathematics as a subject would come on this scale? Would it be more like spellings, where only one correct answer should be given? Or would it be more like art, where learners explain their own unique ways of understanding? Or might it be somewhere in between, requiring some flexibility of thinking but also an understanding that some aspects are a given and cannot be negotiated? Your answers to these questions inform your disposition to teaching mathematics and are likely to influence the way in which you teach it. Being aware of this is a step towards reflective practice when working with young children in a mathematical context.

REFLECTIVE QUESTIONS

Have you thought about the nature of mathematics subject knowledge? When you teach mathematics, do you feel as if you are discovering truths that are 'out there' in the real world? Or do you view mathematics as a human creation, a tool for looking at and explaining the world 'out there'?

Your disposition: mathematics as a human endeavour

The way we view the subject content of mathematics forms the basis of our philosophy of mathematics. You may not have given much consideration to your personal philosophy of mathematics, but the view that you hold can have a significant impact on the pedagogical choices you make. As we have seen, one popular view of the subject content of mathematics is that it is something 'out there' in reality. Mathematical truths are all around us in our environment waiting to be discovered: when we engage in teaching mathematics, we are helping children reach out to ideas that have an existence in the outside world.

In contrast, Lakoff and Nunez (2000) argue that mathematics is in fact a human endeavour created by humans for human purposes. They call mathematics 'a magnificent example of the beauty, richness, complexity, diversity and importance of human ideas. It is a marvellous testament to what the ordinary embodied human mind is capable of – when multiplied by the creative efforts of millions over millennia' (p377). They go on to say that 'human beings have been responsible for the creation of mathematics, and we remain responsible for maintaining and extending it' (p377). In this view, mathematics is not 'out there', but only exists as a function of human thought processes. Mathematics is not 'in' the reality we experience, but is a tool or lens through which we might come to understand reality. Through science and technology, humans have created accurate and refined models for analysing reality, but take away the humans and you take away the mathematics. So, if we were to adopt this view, how might that influence our pedagogical approach to supporting children's early mathematics mastery?

Take, as an example, the number '2'. In the idealist view, two apples have an intrinsic property of 'twoness'. The apples hold the logical properties of the idea '2', and seeing that the apples embody the idea '2', we label the apples '2'. But in the empirical view, the apples never have the property '2'. It is humans that give the apples the label '2'. The apples exist quite happily on their own, but when we see them we notice that they fit our idea of '2' and we choose to label them '2'. In fact, we can apply '2' to two children or two claps, or anything that fits the category '2' which we have created.

If you accept this as an explanation, then young children's mastery of early mathematics is a process of testing out 'thought tools' rather than finding logical truths that are 'out there' in the world. A thought tool is a mathematical idea that I need to bring to concrete, symbolic and abstract experiences to consider whether it has logical validity. Some thought tools such as $3 + 4 = 8$ are perfectly valid to test out, but so far we have never – in our collective experience – found this proposition to be true for the world 'out there'. This should not deter young children from trying out their own thought tools, because the ownership of their own thought tools helps to build their self-confidence in taking multiple approaches to a mathematics problem. Fortunately, many generations of mathematicians have created very effective thought tools that, through their continued use and development, have become the established logical truths in mathematics. But allowing young children to ground their own mathematical thinking in the world 'out there' by testing their thinking in concrete, symbolic and abstract experiences feels very different to an approach that overemphasises the modelling of 'correct' answers.

From this perspective, early mathematics mastery begins to look different to early phonics learning. Although children may fairly quickly come to associate the numeral '2' with the spoken word 'two', there is still much learning that needs to be grounded in reality. Young children may come to ground the concept '2' with two concrete objects, but the possible contexts in which this thought tool could be grounded is much more complex. Even in seemingly simple contexts such as the number '20', the '2' is grounded in a way that is different from its use in '32'. In reading, children are already fluent in the way that contexts (such as other words in a sentence or the referents of sentences) change the meaning of groups of phonemes through their mastery of spoken language. However, in mathematics, young children do not generally have a wide experience of grounding mathematical concepts. Therefore, early mastery of mathematics involves understanding simple concepts and grasping how those simple concepts are grounded in different ways in different contexts. We cannot simply rely on fast-paced rote learning as a pedagogy for mastering early mathematics. Another approach is required.

This alternative approach requires us to view mathematics mastery not as the mastering of a truth that is 'out there', but to view mastery as a fluency in grounding complex mathematical concepts in experience. Lakatos (1976) suggests that mathematics be seen as a human activity created and maintained by humans in much the same way that a language is kept alive by native speakers. From a neurological point of view, Lakoff and Nunez (2000) call this view of mathematics learning 'embodied'; for example, neural connections made in the brain embody the sensory experiences the learner is exposed to. In this view, mathematics learning is not algorithmic in the sense of acquiring sequences of facts, but deeply complex and context-dependent. Not only do the mathematical concepts depend on their mathematical context, but also on the emotional, physical and psychological context in which they are learnt. If these conditions constitute a positive experience of mathematical learning, then this is embodied in the disposition that the child has towards future mathematics learning. Rather than early mastery unlocking increasingly large vistas of logic, in this view, mastery of mathematics in the early years involves ensuring children have a positive experience of the culture of mathematical activity in order to ensure that they feel comfortable with the more complex logical aspects of the subject they will encounter in later curriculum content. In the next section, we will be looking at how we might support the development of such a positive disposition.

CASE STUDY

A cognitive frame for teaching mathematics

A cognitive frame is a mental structure created by past experiences that gives us a point of reference for thinking about the present and the future. As teachers and practitioners, we all enter mathematics teaching with existing dispositions towards the subject and its content. This is created during our own experiences of learning mathematics at school, and is sometimes something we are not conscious of but have hidden in the assumptions and approaches we take to teaching mathematics as adults. In the first mathematics session that I teach with student teachers, we try to unpick our prior experiences as mathematics learners by drawing a stereotypical mathematics teacher in groups. This always produces some amusing but also quite worrying results. In the seven years I have been teaching trainee mathematics teachers, I have kept an informal tally of the positive and negative traits that students talk about. Every year and with every group, the list of negative traits has far outweighed the positive ones, to a ratio of about four to one. Of course, this does not mean that all current mathematics teaching is poor, and the activity deliberately caricatures trainees' experiences in order to provide a discussion point. But it does reveal something about the collective experience of mathematics learning that many of us carry. The key purpose of the activity is to consider what hidden dispositions towards mathematics we might unconsciously have and the potential impact that has on the children we work with. At the end of the first session, all trainees write a short cognitive frame about what kind of a mathematics teacher they want to be, a kind of mantra for positive mathematics teaching. This might be something you consider doing yourself if your more recent experiences of mathematics teaching or learning have not been positive. Try drawing a picture of how a child would currently view you as a mathematics teacher or ask a trusted colleague to do this. In the same way as videoing your interactions with children can be revealing, this could be a good starting point for thinking about what of your past experience of mathematics you are passing on to children.

REFLECTIVE QUESTIONS

How would you describe your disposition towards mathematics? How do you feel physically when you teach? What emotions do certain mathematical concepts give you? Can we all express our mathematical knowledge differently?

Children's disposition and early mathematics mastery

As we have said, by disposition we mean the cognitive, psychological, physical and emotional states that frame activity in a given area. A key aspect of mastery of mathematics in the early years is not just direct understanding of the subject content, but the creation of a positive psychological, physical and emotional disposition towards the culture of mathematics activity, of which the cognitive aspects are a component. This view was shared by the mathematician George Polya. In the 1970s, he suggested that mathematics education should not just be concerned with delivering content, but it has a higher aim that is linked to the role mathematical thinking has in human thinking in general. In an interview, he said mathematics is 'not a spectator sport. To understand mathematics means to be able to do mathematics' (Polya, 2002, p6). And according to Polya, the main tactic for being able to do mathematics is to cultivate the 'right attitude for problems' (p6).

What might a positive disposition towards mathematics in the early years look like? In the final sections of this chapter, we will look at the psychological aspects of teaching and learning early mathematics, including the intrinsic (internal) and extrinsic (external) motivations children experience when engaging in mathematics activities. We will consider the transpersonal (beyond the cognitive) aspects of early mathematics mastery; we will look at the physical context in which mathematics learning takes place and the role that this has in laying the foundations for mastery; and finally, we will look at some practical ways to ground mathematics in concrete models.

REFLECTIVE QUESTIONS

When you are planning, do you spend more time thinking about what you will do, or more time thinking about which resources to provide for the children? If you are being observed or you are observing a lesson, do you feel a need to focus on the product of the lesson or the process in which the children are engaged? Could you justify the learning being deep but lacking 'pace'?

Children's disposition: the influence of context

In his book *Transforming Primary Mathematics*, Mike Askew (2012) explores the social context in which mathematics learning takes place. He argues that every time we engage children in a mathematics activity, we should be focusing not only on what the children are learning, but also on what is actually taking place in a social context: what the children are learning about themselves and others as mathematicians. If children's early experience of mathematics is that the teacher draws on the whiteboard and correct answers are recorded there, then children are learning not just the subject content, but also that *it is controlled by the teacher*. In this way, we address children's extrinsic motivations for learning but tend to neglect the development of children's intrinsic motivation. For young mathematicians to master concepts, they need to view themselves as having agency in their learning. Askew argues that children develop a view of themselves as a mathematician if they have plenty of opportunities to explain their thinking to others. In particular, Askew argues that children need to learn to respect the mathematical views of others, and this includes occasions where other children's answers are 'wrong' or their thinking is different from their own.

Askew (2012) encourages us to view the teaching of mathematics as an activity; for example, that the total experiential context of the learning has an impact on what is learnt (p6). In the classroom, children do not develop mastery dispositions in isolation, but within the social, cultural, physical and historical context in which the learning takes place. Importantly, learning is seen as a constantly emerging and evolving process that does not stop once a problem has been solved, but is dissolved within the context of the activity around it. Askew (2012) talks about each class of learners having a 'local history' of learning (p16), a similar concept to the community of memory (Bellah et al., 1985). In practical terms, this means encouraging children to talk about and actively recall the types of learning that have occurred in specific times and places – situating their learning within its context.

Here is an example from my own mathematics teaching where the children and I developed our own vocabulary for the features of a number line. As I was drawing a number line on the whiteboard, one child asked what the name for the marks that segment the line was. Not knowing the answer, we decided as a group to call them 'blips' and the marks at the beginning and end of the line 'buffers'. This developed into a train metaphor and I moved cubes up and down the line as I modelled addition. This kind of learning occurred in a group (community), with the input of the children as well as the adult (agency), and made sense of other resources at hand (the cubes). When we next worked with number lines and cubes, I actively encouraged the children to recall when, where and what we had agreed as a group when we 'invented' the train metaphor, placing the mathematics activity within its context (the history of the learning).

REFLECTIVE QUESTIONS

Are you aware of the schemas of young children? Have you considered how you might add mathematical content to these schemas? When you are planning and delivering mathematics activities, do you consider the context in which the learning takes place?

Thinking about pedagogy: from schemas to conceptual metaphors

Athey (2007) provides a useful conceptual framework for identifying and supporting young children's learning through the use of schemas. Schemas are 'patterns of behaviour and thinking in children that exist underneath the surface features of various contents, contexts and specific experiences' (Athey, 2007, p5). As we watch young children engaging in purposeful play, we are able to observe repetitions, habits and motifs that represent early learning at a conceptual level. For example, a dynamic vertical schema might be illustrated by repeatedly climbing up ladders, drawing towers, making towers with blocks, or watching water fountains. Teachers and practitioners who identify these schemas are then able to nourish this play with worthwhile content (Nutbrown, 2011, p14) such as early counting skills. This approach effectively develops child-initiated learning and encourages children's intrinsic motivation to participate in mathematics activity. But how do we nourish these schemas with content? One possible approach is to view mathematical concepts as metaphors.

Lakoff and Nunez (2000) argue that the whole of mathematics can be viewed as a series of metaphors about the world: mathematics is literally a metaphorical language that is used to describe the phenomena we experience on a daily basis. In mathematics, the most common conceptual metaphors are grounding metaphors, which can be checked through direct concrete experiences ('there are three apples' can be checked by counting the real apples), and linking metaphors, which link one abstract concept to another (the numbers on a number track have the same order as numbers on a number line). In the early years, most of the conceptual metaphors that children encounter will be grounding metaphors that effectively label objects in the environment ('there are four slices of cake') or processes that occur in the environment ('one slice of cake out of the four is eaten'). In the same way that schemas of behaviour can be repeated in different contexts (e.g. climbing up ladders, climbing up trees, toys climbing the stairs), so grounding metaphors can be applied to different experiences. The number 'four' can be a metaphor for the number of children in a line, the days until my birthday, or the number of rewards I have been given; the calculation $4 - 1 = 3$ can be a metaphor for apples in a basket, jobs I have completed or chairs at a table. Mathematics mastery in the early years thus involves the applications of as many grounding metaphors to as many contexts as possible.

The use of grounding metaphors also has an emotional aspect that must be understood in order to support young children's disposition towards these basic concepts. Lakoff and Nunez (2000) use the word 'conflation' (p42) to describe the neural connections made in the brain when two different kinds of experience occur inseparably at the same time. In this process, two parts of the brain are activated and generate a single experience. An awareness of conflation is a very important aspect of supporting mastery of grounding metaphors. For example, the calculation $4 - 1 = 3$ can be used as a grounding metaphor for a cake sliced into four pieces from which one piece has been eaten. We can check the truth of this with children by actually slicing a cake into four pieces and then eating one piece. Children may well experience a sense of loss or hunger during the process of you eating the cake slice. Loss and the grounding metaphor of the subtraction calculation activate two separate parts of brain activity (an emotion and a logical agreement) that come together to generate one experience. As a result, the process of subtraction could, in this case, simultaneously give rise to the experience of loss.

So, while schemas lack content, grounding metaphors are rich in contextual meaning in addition to their logical and metaphorical content. Just as we would scaffold children's schemas by providing opportunities for experiencing them in different contexts, so we should scaffold children's experiences of grounding metaphors by considering the psychological and emotional context in which the learning is taking place. To counter a feeling of loss becoming associated with all subtraction calculations, children could experience the positive emotions of ticking one job off a list of four jobs. The grounding metaphor stays the same but has a different context, and we would want to encourage the children to talk about their emotional reactions to both scenarios. The concept of conflation is also particularly important in relation to the way a group of learners experiences mathematics as a subject. If a teacher harshly reprimands a child for an incorrect answer, the incorrect answer and the emotion become one experience for the individual child. But even for those children who did not give an incorrect answer, the association of mathematics activity in general and negative emotions may become established. As teachers and practitioners, we should be aware of the subtle contextual associations of mathematics learning in order to ensure that the most positive dispositions are developed.

RESEARCH

Transpersonal theory

'Transpersonal' is a term used to define phenomena that relate to experiences beyond the ego or the cognitive functioning of humans. Mathematics has traditionally been viewed as an egocentric subject in which only the cognitive aspects are considered during the teaching and learning of the subject content. In contrast to this approach, Ferrer (2017) suggests the *equiprimacy principle*, 'according to which no human attribute is intrinsically superior or more evolved than any other' (p11). That means psychological, physical and emotional attributes have an equal role in learning to the brain-centred cognitive aspects. In order to develop children's positive disposition for later mathematics mastery, we could consider more than just the cognitive aspects of mathematics learning (epitomised by the rote learning of mathematical facts). Braud (2006) argues that 'knowledge is empty unless it is connected internally with what is known' (p135). In other words, to master a subject, we could embrace the equiprimacy principle. Indeed, many professional mathematicians talk of experiencing numbers as colours or in seeing an inherent beauty in number sequences. In this sense, their understanding incorporates knowledge that goes beyond cognitive functioning to include a felt sense of mathematical concepts.

REFLECTIVE QUESTIONS

Do you see finger-counting as a preparatory stage for understanding the number sequence and seek to encourage children to move beyond it as soon as possible? Do you vary the way that you use your fingers to count and model this to children? Have you ever noticed children using their fingers to count in a different way? Did you encourage and share this with other children?

Thinking about pedagogy: grounding mathematical metaphors

The equiprimacy principle is generally already utilised in early years mathematics, where the fingers are widely used to support early counting, addition and subtraction. There is good reason to use this approach with young children as it has been found that well-established neural pathways connect the fingertips to the brain, and so engaging this in the learning process builds on existing neural connections. However, generally speaking, only one approach to using the fingers is common in Western culture: start with the thumb of either hand and move sequentially to the left or right (see Figure 4.1).

This is an effective way of learning the number sequence but also of establishing the cardinality of numbers; for example, if I start from my right-hand thumb, then I quickly learn that the little finger of the right hand always represents the number 'five'. However, if we only ever introduce this one model of finger-counting, we are in effect viewing the use of the body as a preparatory stage to counting on number tracks and number lines. In this sense, we might try to move children as quickly as possible on to more abstract counting and calculation tools. For mastery of a concept, we are interested in different ways of representing the same mathematical concept, so the following are some alternative ways in which the fingers can be used for counting.

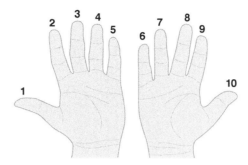

Figure 4.1   A sequential approach to finger-counting

By placing both hands with the palms facing up and little fingers close together, we can use a slightly different counting sequence. We can start with the left thumb, then count the right thumb, then count the left index finger, then the right index finger, and so on (see Figure 4.2).

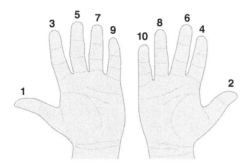

Figure 4.2   A 'butterfly' approach to finger-counting

This sequence of counting still only uses the numbers to ten, but the sequence 'feels' different. Children tend to like the sense of symmetry that this sequence instils, and one child that I worked with called it 'butterfly' counting because the fingers gradually unfurl on each hand like the wings of a butterfly opening. This counting sequence also provides a grounding metaphor for odd and even numbers. Once you have counted to ten, all of the fingers on the left hand are odd and all of the fingers on the right hand are even. It is also a grounding metaphor for double numbers: both thumbs being the same as double one, both index fingers being the same as double two, and so on.

These first two methods of counting tend to emphasise the conceptual metaphor of base 10 counting systems; for example, we have to do something different (add an extra pair of hands) if we want to count beyond ten. However, there are finger-counting systems that allow grounding of other mathematical number concepts. In the Babylonian number-counting system, you start with the left hand. The thumb is the counting/pointing finger and we begin by touching the base of the left index finger – this is one. Next we touch the middle division of the index finger – this is two. Then we touch the top of the index finger – this is three (see Figure 4.3).

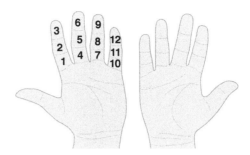

Figure 4.3   A Babylonian approach to finger-counting

Teaching this system alongside the traditional finger-counting system has a number of benefits in terms of mastery of the grounding metaphor of counting. First, there is a natural grouping of numbers into threes (one finger = a count of three), which supports the development of the grouping objects grounding metaphor. Second, this system is a base 12 counting system because you need to do something different (raise a finger on your right hand) when you reach 12 and want to carry on counting. This is a most useful link to working with analogue and digital clocks where the number 12 signals the completion of half of a day-long cycle. On an analogue clock face, the hour numbers 1, 2 and 3 appear in the first quarter, just as they appear on the first finger; 4, 5 and 6 appear in the second quarter and on the second finger. Much later, when it comes to the mastery of angles, the base 12 counting system is used to split the 360-degree circle up into smaller units, and again this system supports the understanding of that grounding metaphor.

A final counting system that may be of some use is the Chinese finger-counting system. In this approach, you start with the index finger of the right hand. You then count to the left until you reach four (the little finger), and then the placeholder is the thumb (five). Six, seven and eight then follow in sequence, with the thumb as a placeholder. In this sense, this is a base 5 counting system (see Figure 4.4).

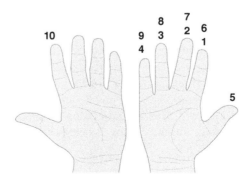

Figure 4.4   A Chinese approach to finger-counting

I have found that some children take to this counting system naturally, while others struggle, particularly when using it to add numbers together. It has the advantage that all of the numbers up to 59 can be counted using just two hands (and further if you incorporate each of the sections of the fingers), and the system is used widely in China to support children's mental mathematics. Aside from these benefits, it can also be used to illustrate that not all mathematical concepts originated in the West – the Eurocentric view that all mathematical concepts were discovered by Europeans (Noyes, 2007). Mathematics has a tendency to disenfranchise children's mathematical cultural heritage, and sharing the historical origins of mathematical discoveries can enable children to reconnect with their mathematical cultural history and safeguard their mathematical cultural identity. Hopefully, in these examples, you can begin to get the idea that early mastery of a range of finger-counting supports understanding of an associated range of grounding metaphors. It also provides a useful illustration of the conditionality of counting: the number three can be illustrated in more than one way, and therefore there is not one 'correct' answer to 'Show me three on your fingers'.

CHAPTER SUMMARY

Key points covered in this chapter are:

- an empirical view of mathematics that encourages us to view mathematics as a human creation and support young children's mastery of mathematics by inviting them into this cultural endeavour;

- the idea that the context in which mathematics learning takes place can help or hinder young mathematicians' perception of the subject in complex but important ways;

- a way of moving from the identification of young children's mathematical schemas towards the scaffolding of simple mathematical concepts to support the journey to mastery;

- the use of the body as an important dimension in mastery of mathematics, including an awareness of emotions during mathematics activity and the direct use of the physical body to understand multiple representations of concepts.

Further reading

Askew, M. (2012) *Transforming Primary Mathematics*. London: Routledge.

This book looks in detail at the implications of viewing mathematics learning as an activity situated within a learning context. It is both accessible and profound, and may change the way you view mathematics teaching.

Ferrer, J., Romero, M. and Albareda, R. (2005) 'Integral transformative education: a participatory approach'. *Journal of Transformative Education*, 3(4): 306–30.

Although this paper relates to teaching and learning in higher education, it provides a thought-provoking portrait of integral education that considers all aspects of human engagement in the learning process. It is particularly relevant to discussion of mastery as it favours depth of understanding over breadth of understanding.

Lakoff, G. and Nunez, R. (2000) *Where Mathematics Comes From: How the Embodied Mind Brings Mathematics into Being*. New York: Basic Books.

This philosophical book provides an alternative view of mathematics as a vast construction of conceptual metaphors. In meticulous detail, it covers the way in which simple mathematical ideas are composed of grounded and linking metaphors, but it is also easy to dip into for inspiration.

References

Askew, M. (2012) *Transforming Primary Mathematics*. London: Routledge.

Athey, C. (2007) *Extending Thought in Young Children: A Parent–Teacher Partnership*, 2nd edn. London: SAGE.

Bellah, R., Madsen, W., Sullivan, W., Swidler, A. and Tipton, S. (1985) *Habits of the Heart: Individualism and Commitment in American Life*. New York: Harper & Row.

Braud, W. (2006) 'Education and the "more" in holistic transpersonal higher education: a 30+ year perspective on the approach of the Institute of Transpersonal Psychology'. *Journal of Transpersonal Psychology*, 38(2): 133–58.

Ferrer, J. (2017) *Participation and the Mystery: Transpersonal Essays in Psychology, Education and Religion*. Albany, NY: SUNY Press.

Getzels, J. and Thelen, H. (1972) 'A conceptual framework for the study of the classroom group as a social system'. In A. Morrison and D. McIntyre (eds), *The Social Psychology of Teaching*. Middlesex: Penguin Education, pp17–34.

Lakatos, I. (ed.) (1976) *Proofs and Refutations: The Logics of Mathematical Discovery*. Cambridge: Cambridge University Press.

Lakoff, G. and Nunez, R. (2000) *Where Mathematics Comes From: How the Embodied Mind Brings Mathematics into Being*. New York: Basic Books.

Noss, R. and Hoyles, C. (1996) 'The visibility of meanings: modelling the mathematics of banking'. *International Journal of Computers for Mathematical Learning*, 1(1): 3–31.

Noyes, A. (2007) *Rethinking School Mathematics*. London: Paul Chapman Publishing.

Nutbrown, C. (2011) *Threads of Thinking: Schemas and Young Children's Learning*. London: SAGE.

Polya, G. (2002) *The Goals of Mathematical Education Part 1*. Available at: www.educ.fc.ul.pt/docentes/jponte/fdm/textos/Polya%202007a.pdf

5

SUBJECT KNOWLEDGE

ROSALYN HYDE, LOUISE HOSKYNS-STAPLES AND MARY O'CONNOR

KEYWORDS: TEACHER BELIEFS; MODELS AND REPRESENTATIONS; PLANNING; COHERENCE; DEVELOPING SUBJECT KNOWLEDGE

CHAPTER OBJECTIVES

This chapter will allow you to achieve the following outcomes:

- develop an understanding of some of the key features of good subject knowledge;
- appreciate the importance of good subject knowledge at all levels;
- understand how to improve your subject knowledge for teaching mathematics.

Introduction

To improve mathematics education for students, an important action that should be taken is improving the quality of their teachers' knowledge of school mathematics.

(Ma, 2010, p123)

The chapter will explore some of the questions that using mastery approaches raise regarding subject knowledge for teachers of mathematics. Boylan et al. (2017) identify both teacher beliefs and weak subject knowledge as barriers to the implementation of the mastery approaches being promoted by the National Centre for Excellence in the Teaching of Mathematics (NCETM) in England. Studies of both primary and secondary teachers cited by Zhang and Wong (2015) identify that many mathematics teachers 'do not consistently possess sufficient subject knowledge for effective mathematics teaching' (p466). Zhang and Wong (2015) also find that the literature suggests poor teacher subject knowledge can lead to poor pedagogical content knowledge. The chapter discusses the depth and connectedness of understanding needed by teachers of mathematics as well as the importance of beliefs, and identifies some ways that teachers can develop their mathematics subject knowledge.

RESEARCH

The need for a profound understanding of fundamental mathematics

The false assumption that teaching elementary mathematics is superficial because of the content involved is challenged in the work of Ma (2010), who describes a highly sophisticated subject knowledge.

Her in-depth study revealed a coherence in the knowledge of Chinese teachers who constantly sought to explain why something makes sense mathematically. This allowed them to go deeper in exploring conceptual understanding and to make connections between concepts as a result. In this way, they formed what Ma (2010) refers to as 'knowledge packages', structures of interlinking concepts formed by each teacher in considering how a mathematical concept could be systematically revealed to learners in a meaningful way. The structure of these packages involves a central sequence of concepts that develop with the support of other linked concepts. Within each knowledge package, some concepts are considered 'key' because of their significance to the learning of the concept. Figure 5.1 shows a knowledge package for subtraction with regrouping where the shaded concepts are the 'key pieces'.

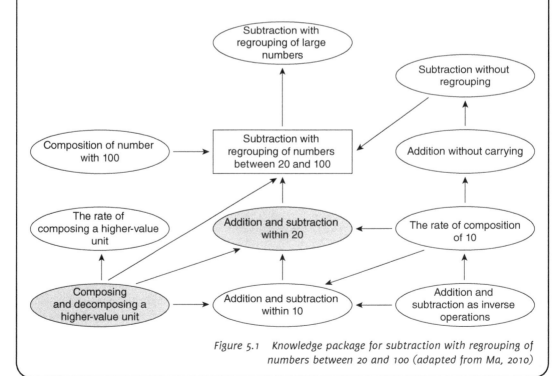

Figure 5.1   Knowledge package for subtraction with regrouping of numbers between 20 and 100 (adapted from Ma, 2010)

Chinese teachers believed that the sequence of concepts was important in developing their learners' knowledge and skills. The underpinning philosophy is not too dissimilar to that maintained by the NCETM (2017) in its concept of mastery teaching and the notion that 'small steps are easier to take'.

According to Ma (2010), when knowledge packages combine, they help to form a solid network of subject matter knowledge, referred to as a profound understanding of fundamental mathematics (PUFM). This is an extensive knowledge that has much depth as well as breadth of school mathematics, and includes other aspects such as the teacher's attitudes towards its teaching and learning. Teachers achieving PUFM also maintained four specific properties within their teaching:

- *Connectedness*, which involves the teacher deliberately exploring in their planning, and exposing in their teaching, mathematical connections in order to provide a cohesive learning that aims to restrict the extent to which topics are learnt in isolation.

- The *multiple perspectives* property concerns teachers' appreciation for the differences that exist in mathematics which generate different ideas and solutions. A teacher with PUFM appreciates their advantages and disadvantages, and can explain the differences in a way that allows learners to achieve a flexible understanding.

- A teacher achieving PUFM also has a comprehensive awareness of the *basic ideas* behind a concept. These simple concepts are powerful, holding the key to understanding, and are therefore revised frequently.

- The last property is that of *longitudinal coherence*, which is knowledge and understanding of the entire elementary curriculum, not just of the year that is being taught. Revision of previously learnt important concepts can easily become commonplace, and the foundations are securely laid for learning in subsequent years.

Ma (2010) observes how Chinese teachers' subject and pedagogical knowledge is supported by the nature of school mathematics. This is a reciprocal relationship as high-quality school mathematics stems from high-quality teacher knowledge, or PUFM. Supporting teachers in comprehensively developing a form of PUFM, within a mastery approach, is a major step in reforming mathematics teaching.

Features of mastery

Chapter 1 in this book defines what we mean by mastery and describes its key features. In this section, aspects of mastery are considered in terms of the demands on teachers' subject knowledge in order to facilitate children learning mathematics with the fluency, reasoning and problem-solving skills required in the English National Curriculum (DfE, 2014). In broad terms, a mastery approach intends that learners develop a coherent view of mathematics, are able to reason mathematically, have both conceptual understanding and procedural fluency, are confident problem-solvers, and are able to use skills of generalisation. It is difficult to see how it would be possible for learners to develop these skills unless their teachers already have these skills themselves. However, while good subject knowledge is a necessary condition for good teaching, it is not sufficient in that it does not automatically mean that teaching is of a high standard. Shao et al. (2013) describe teaching mathematics as a 'fine balance' between '"extensive practice" and understanding; variant embodiments and invariant "essence"; guidance and self-exploration; explanative analysis and exploratory exercise; and logical induction and inductive synthesis' (p23). Fine balance requires good knowledge and understanding in order to exercise such judgement.

Essential to good mathematics teaching is the teacher's personal knowledge of the connections within and between mathematics topics, and their ability to identify necessary prior learning and the small steps through which learning progresses – in other words, to be able to structure and sequence learning meaningfully for learners.

As identified previously, Ma (2010) found that the Chinese teachers she interviewed had what she calls 'knowledge packages', which, for a particular topic, identify all the topics that support – or are supported by – the topic and the relationships between them. She further says that a fully developed and well-organised knowledge package contains procedural topics, conceptual topics and basic principles. Figure 5.2 shows the knowledge package for multiplication by two-digit numbers.

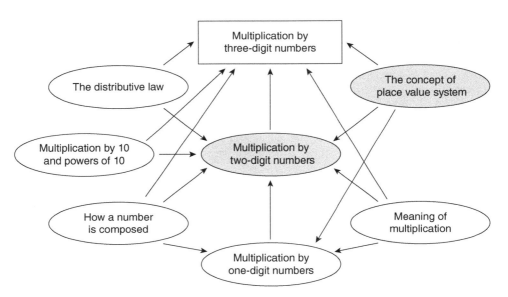

Figure 5.2   A knowledge package for multiplication by two-digit numbers (adapted from Ma, 2010)

In the case of multiplication by three-digit numbers, it is striking that the Chinese teachers are reported as identifying the key learning as being multiplication by two-digit numbers and multiplication by three-digit numbers as an extension of that. The knowledge packages also make it clear that the Chinese teachers had a clear understanding as to what constitutes the first and smallest step in learning a new topic. Ma (2010) goes on to say that teachers pay particular attention to the teaching of an idea in its simplest form when it is first encountered in order to provide a secure basis for later learning, which will also reinforce the earlier learning. Part of being able to 'master' mathematics is to know alternative ways to solve a problem, to be able to explain why a method works, and to be able to identify the most elegant and efficient way of solving a particular problem.

Alcock (2017) suggests that human beings have an inherent ability to look for commonalities between experiences in order to make them predictable – in other words, to generalise. Generalising is at the heart of mathematical thinking because mathematics both makes sense and is about sense-making. However, when learners find patterns where they do not exist, or find them too hastily, they can form incorrect, or partially incorrect, conceptions of mathematics. Alcock (2017) contends that for young learners, 'it is not obvious what is a key property for a mathematical object and what is incidental' (pp22–3). A skilled mathematics teacher is able to use their own personal subject knowledge, along with their other skills, to identify the potential misconceptions learners might have about a topic and decide how to best utilise those in their teaching. Hence, a good teacher makes careful choices in terms of the sequencing of learning, choices of representations and of examples and problems. It takes a skilled teacher not to inadvertently mislead learners or reinforce precisely the misconceptions they are trying to avoid. The structure that makes two mathematics problems similar in some way is also not always obvious to learners; this is the purpose of variation in teaching mathematics where purposeful change is made in order to expose aspects of the mathematics being learnt. However, it is difficult to see how a teacher might support learners in understanding the structures underpinning mathematics if they do not understand themselves.

REFLECTIVE QUESTIONS

What features of mastery are present in your own teaching? Which would you like to develop?

Coherence, connectedness and small steps

Underpinning mathematics are some powerful conceptual ideas. These are sometimes called 'big ideas' in mathematics (Fujita and Hyde, 2014). Ideas such as place value are related to the structure of mathematics and support a number of other, different mathematics topics. When preparing to teach a topic, teachers need to consider which aspects of mathematics are connected to the topic; for example, place value and the composition of a number in the example of three-digit multiplication (see Figure 5.2). Some of these aspects will be prerequisites for the new learning and others will enable learners to make useful longer-term links in their understanding. For example, to understand fractions, a learner needs knowledge of division; the understanding developed in learning about fractions will support future learning about ratio. Each of these three topics requires multiplicative reasoning.

The need for a careful sequence of lessons to ensure that learners develop the correct understanding of a concept is discussed above and explored in more detail later in this chapter. Ma (2010) demonstrates how Chinese teachers consider all of the areas of mathematical knowledge that are required by learners to enable them to understand a topic. This 'unpacking' of the 'compressed' mathematical knowledge that adults have developed, and eventually learners need, requires very careful attention on the part of the teacher to the subject knowledge and learning required for each concept (Edwards et al., 2015). Considering the 'small steps' required in the learning to build the concept is one way to 'unpack' the knowledge and develop a coherent sequence of learning within a lesson and between lessons. The learning within each lesson should overlap with the following lesson, enabling learners to build on their learning in incremental steps. The links between each step need to be carefully considered, otherwise there is the potential for 'fragmenting the mathematics into [small] disconnected pieces' (Boylan et al., 2019, p17).

An example of coherent small steps within a lesson on comparing fractions could be as follows:

1. Ask learners to predict what will happen when the numerator is either increased or decreased but the denominator stays the same (the *number* of parts is getting bigger or smaller). For example, Caan has $\frac{3}{5}$ of a bar of chocolate and John has $\frac{4}{5}$ of a bar; who has the most?

2. Provide opportunities for learners to use a range of representations (e.g. a cut-up fraction wall, some bars of chocolate, or to find the positions of the fractions on a number line or draw a bar model).

3. Share the findings of the class and check if their conjectures proved to be true.

The next series of steps repeats the above stages but keeps the numerator the same and changes the denominator (the *size* of the parts is getting bigger or smaller). For example, Caan has $\frac{3}{5}$ of a bar of chocolate and Mae has $\frac{3}{4}$ of a bar; who has the most?

1. What do learners notice about the relationship between the numerator and the denominator?

2. Learners share their ideas regarding both numerators and denominators.

3. Can they predict who has the most chocolate between John and Mae, and can they show this using the representations used throughout the lesson?

Each time, the learner only needs to attend to one aspect of the fraction. Developing the learning like this supports a deep understanding of each aspect of the mathematics. What is taught in each lesson needs to be carefully structured so that the key point for the lesson can be understood by all.

REFLECTIVE QUESTION

Try writing a series of small steps for a topic you are going to teach. What are the essential elements for conceptual learning?

Manipulatives, models and representations

There are lots of manipulatives, models and representations available to teachers of mathematics. Concrete materials (manipulatives) are valuable for all learners, and particularly for those learners with additional needs who may have a lower working memory, higher levels of mathematics anxiety and longer processing times for learning (Needham, 2018). There are lots of mathematical pedagogical tools teachers can choose from to support learners (e.g. place value cards, counters, algebra tiles, bar models, Numicon, bead strings, Dienes apparatus, Cuisenaire rods). Because different representations expose different misconceptions and can be used to develop different aspects of understanding for any particular concept, teachers need to make choices about the manipulatives, representations and models they use with learners. The use of diagrams is a powerful problem-solving strategy (Henderson et al., 2017).

Learners will also develop their use of models and representations, favouring more powerful and generalised models, as they progress in understanding of a particular concept. The concrete–pictorial–abstract (CPA) approach that is universally used in Singapore and forms part of the NCETM mastery approach is based on the work of Bruner (1966). At primary school level, a CPA approach might mean starting with the physical object to manipulate, moving to pictorial representations of the object, and then to manipulatives such as cubes, before moving to diagrams and then to more abstract representations such as number sentences using digits. Conversely, the use of manipulatives can also be used to explain the abstract. Manipulatives are of value for learners of all ages, and should act as a scaffold as ideas and concepts are understood and developed (Henderson et al., 2017). Learners should be looking to use powerful models and representations that offer opportunities to generalise, to connect new learning to previous learning, and that expose the structure of new ideas and problems.

The following example explores a number of different models and representations for sharing an amount in a given ratio. Erin and Mary share 12 sweets in the ratio 1:2. How many sweets does each of them have?

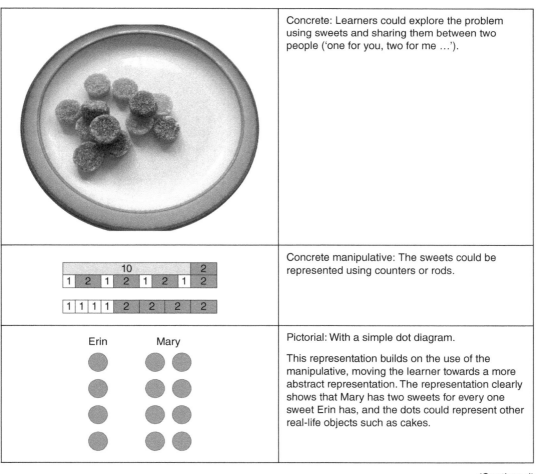

	Concrete: Learners could explore the problem using sweets and sharing them between two people ('one for you, two for me …').
	Concrete manipulative: The sweets could be represented using counters or rods.
Erin Mary	Pictorial: With a simple dot diagram. This representation builds on the use of the manipulative, moving the learner towards a more abstract representation. The representation clearly shows that Mary has two sweets for every one sweet Erin has, and the dots could represent other real-life objects such as cakes.

(Continued)

(Continued)

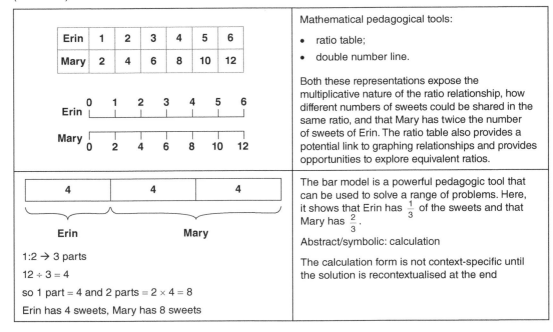

	Mathematical pedagogical tools:
(Erin/Mary ratio table and double number line diagrams)	• ratio table; • double number line. Both these representations expose the multiplicative nature of the ratio relationship, how different numbers of sweets could be shared in the same ratio, and that Mary has twice the number of sweets of Erin. The ratio table also provides a potential link to graphing relationships and provides opportunities to explore equivalent ratios.
(bar model diagram with Erin and Mary) 1:2 → 3 parts 12 ÷ 3 = 4 so 1 part = 4 and 2 parts = 2 × 4 = 8 Erin has 4 sweets, Mary has 8 sweets	The bar model is a powerful pedagogic tool that can be used to solve a range of problems. Here, it shows that Erin has $\frac{1}{3}$ of the sweets and that Mary has $\frac{2}{3}$. Abstract/symbolic: calculation The calculation form is not context-specific until the solution is recontextualised at the end

Importantly, Bruner (1966) was not proposing that there was a unique representation for each concept, but that the role of the teacher is to make an appropriate choice of representation based on considerations of *economy* and *power*. Leong et al. (2015) argue that what is considered 'concrete', 'pictorial' or 'abstract' is not fixed, and therefore the role of the teacher is to 'calibrate the modes to suit the needs of their students' (p11). Such decisions by the teacher require good subject knowledge in order to take into account the age and degree of mathematical understanding held by learners.

REFLECTIVE QUESTIONS

What manipulatives, models and representations are useful in teaching particular topics in mathematics? How does the teacher choose which one to use?

Language in teaching mathematics

Both teaching and learning mathematics make considerable demands on the language capabilities of the teacher and of the learner. In terms of vocabulary, there are words that are only used in mathematics (such as trapezium), words that have common meanings in both the mathematics register and common language, and words that have a distinct meaning in mathematics that differs from their common meaning. Examples of the latter would be words such as 'similar', 'significant' and 'identity'. There are also alternative words used for the same mathematical operation; for example, 'difference' (a word with a specific mathematical meaning compared to its common usage), 'take away' and 'subtract'. Mathematics also has its own syntax, and there are specific ways in which mathematics is both written and read; for example, connectives such as 'if' and 'then' have specific meanings in the syntax of mathematics. In mathematics, symbols form part of the writing. When mathematicians solve a problem, what they write is usually precise and symbol-dense but also complete and understandable by another mathematician. Describing a mathematics problem in words requires an exceptional level of precision, and this sometimes makes writing wordy questions challenging for novice teachers. 'Explaining' can mean something different in mathematics from common language, because in mathematics a calculation can be an explanation. All these issues require good mathematics subject knowledge and skill on the part of the teacher in order to communicate effectively to learners, as well as to support learners in developing the skills to communicate mathematics effectively.

One notable feature of East Asian mathematics teaching is the high level of precision in the language used by both teachers and learners. Shao et al. (2013) identify the important components of teacher exposition as concision and precision. They describe being concise as meaning that teaching is effective and precise. Precise is not taken to mean brief, but that the teacher focuses on the essential content, the important points, and takes into account learners' understanding when identifying the key points to highlight. This precision and concision is also taken further to include being profound, thorough and accurate in developing learners' knowledge. Primary teachers on the Department for Education (DfE)/NCETM China–England exchange programme identified the precise use of mathematical language as a feature of the pedagogy they observed, and that this was one aspect of their experience that was readily adopted by exchange participants (Boylan et al., 2018). They further identify one of the practices implemented following the exchange as being teachers modelling the use of precise mathematical language and encouraging learners to respond to questions using full sentences and correct language (Boylan et al., 2019). Chen and Li (2010) make explicit that teachers' use of mathematical language should include clearly pointing out relationships between parts of the lesson, and the language teachers use plays an important role in this.

Until recently, it would have been uncommon in England for primary-age learners to be familiar with words such as 'commutative', 'associative' and 'distributive'. That teachers may not know and understand this vocabulary is implied by Alcock (2017) when she infers that such vocabulary is generally encountered by mathematics students at university level. An increased focus by primary teachers on using correct mathematical language by both themselves and learners requires secondary school teachers to 'up their game' and to understand and use mathematical language with at least the same level of precision. This is a challenge for those who either did not learn their own mathematics in this way or who are non-specialist teachers of mathematics.

REFLECTIVE QUESTION

If increased precision in language is considered to be a good pedagogical approach, when might it be appropriate to introduce terminology: at the beginning of a topic to thoroughly embed it, or when some learning has taken place and the vocabulary can be understood?

Planning and sequencing learning

One of the differences in the structure of lessons in Shanghai compared to typical lessons in England is that lessons stem from a problem rather than from lesson objectives (Boylan et al., 2019), where the problem might be a 'real-life' situation and is returned to at the end of the lesson. As previously mentioned, another notable feature of mathematics lessons in Shanghai are the small steps in learning planned for by teachers, with a focus on one key point in each lesson; these are key features of the coherence promoted by the NCETM (2017) as one of their 'big ideas of mastery'. Teaching through the use of small steps need not be confused with 'spoon-feeding'; the small steps allow learners to do the thinking and for the vast majority of the class to make progress together. Learning mathematics as a meaningful activity requires the teacher to identify these steps in the learning in order to form a coherent 'journey' or 'story', whereas spoon-feeding is providing learners with each step but not requiring them to attend to the mathematics being learnt.

This chapter identifies coherence and connectedness as features of good mathematics teaching, as well as the need for teachers to exercise 'fine judgement'. Coherence and connectedness in mathematics lessons does not happen by accident; it needs planning for, especially in order that they form part of the experience of learners. Fine judgement is exercised by teachers in planning as well as teaching. Ding et al.'s (2013) work on Chinese teachers' use of textbooks finds four aspects to lesson planning:

a) *identifying the important and difficult points of teaching,*

b) *studying the purposes of each worked example and practice problem,*

c) *exploring the reasons behind certain textbook information,*

d) *exploring the best approaches to present examples from the perspectives of students.*

(p76)

All of these suggest that planning for mathematics learning is a highly skilled, time-consuming activity, but one that can significantly impact on learners' understanding. As Ding et al. (2013) make clear, planning for learning not only involves identifying what learning is going to take place, but also identifying and preparing resources for learning. Also, key in planning for learning is developing effective use of variation (see also Chapter 1). Following their own research on variation, Watson and Mason (2006) conclude that 'control of dimensions of variation and ranges of change is a powerful design strategy for producing exercises that encourage learners to engage with mathematical structure, to generalize and to conceptualize even when doing apparently mundane questions' (pp108–9). This leads them to suggest a skilled process of planning teaching sequences by going through the steps of analysing concepts, identifying regularities, identifying exemplifying variations, constructing exercises, and developing micro-modelling sequences (Watson and Mason, 2006).

As an example, consider the topic of perimeter, area and volume at Key Stage 3. A good place to start is to identify what learners have previously encountered in the topic at Key Stage 2. Looking at schemes of work, the National Curriculum (DfE, 2014), national tests and other sources of information identifies that learners should already be able to measure and calculate the perimeter of composite rectilinear shapes and solve problems using this knowledge.

Using the National Curriculum (DfE, 2014), the new knowledge at Key Stage 3 is identified as calculating and solving problems involving perimeters of triangles, parallelograms and trapezia and calculating and solving problems involving perimeters of two-dimensional shapes (including circles) and composite shapes. Learners will need to use the properties of polygons to help them with the first part and develop an understanding of π as the ratio of the diameter and circumference of a circle for the second.

The secondary mastery professional development materials for Key Stage 3 from the NCETM (2019) identify six mathematical themes for the curriculum along with associated core concepts, 'knowledge, skills and understanding' statements, and key ideas for each of these themes. These materials are intended to support departments with planning and provide teachers with help in breaking down topics in this way. Returning to the perimeter example, Figure 5.3 shows these elements for this topic in a diagrammatic form. The key to sequencing learning is to identify the conceptual steps in learning in order to develop understanding, rather than focusing on processes and procedures.

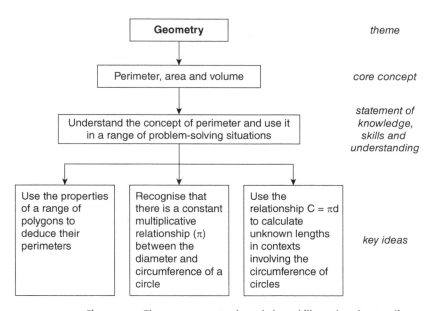

Figure 5.3   Themes, concepts, knowledge, skills and understanding, and key ideas for perimeter (developed from NCETM, 2019)

The importance of teacher beliefs

Ernest (1989) acknowledged that in addition to subject knowledge, teacher beliefs account for differences between how mathematics teachers teach the subject. Zhang and Wong (2015) also suggest that the beliefs teachers have about mathematics and mathematics teaching can strongly influence how effectively they teach, which in turn influences the learning that takes place within their classroom. Zhang and Wong (2015) also believe that a mathematics teacher will already possess a set of beliefs and myths about mathematics before entering the classroom. Holm and Kajander (2012) found that subject knowledge and beliefs are not segregated; they are intrinsically combined, where teachers with identical subject knowledge may create completely different classroom environments for their learners based on their beliefs, ranging from using problem-solving approaches to using a didactic teaching approach.

The complexity of the internal beliefs that teachers hold, be it memories of their own inspirational teachers or the image of themselves as an effective teacher, all contribute to the attitudes, personal experience and expectations that make up a complex web of beliefs which are difficult to define (Kagan, 1992; Thompson, 1992). This is particularly relevant in mathematics classrooms as the perceived difficulties of the subject relate to the beliefs of teachers who consider some mathematics topics are beyond the scope of their subject knowledge.

Ernest (1989) considers three different beliefs about the nature of teaching mathematics: first, the 'problem-solving view', where mathematics is believed to expand a field of human inquiry as an unfinished product; second, the 'Platonist view', where mathematics is believed to be a static but unified body of connected knowledge; and third, the 'instrumentalist view', where mathematics is believed to be a useful – but unrelated – collection of rules and facts (p21). He further defined three distinct roles for mathematics teachers: the instructor, with focus based on skills and mastery; the explainer, focusing on conceptual understanding; and the facilitator, building confident problem-solving. Askew et al. (1997) called these three approaches transmission, discovery and connectionist (p29).

Ball (1990) argues that novice teachers need to unlearn what they know about mathematics from school and university courses to develop their self-awareness and beliefs. Similarly, Beswick (2012) avers that attention needs to be paid to beliefs about the nature of mathematics beginning teachers construct on the basis of their personal learning experiences. Beswick et al. (2012) suggest that beliefs are acted upon as knowledge, becoming crucial in shaping classroom practice, arguing it is teachers' beliefs about mathematics teaching and learning, rather than the nature of approaches to teaching, that matter to students' learning. Schoenfeld (1994) suggests that 'mathematics is an inherently social activity' (p60), yet he found learners often consider mathematics to be a received body of knowledge. Borko et al. (1992) note that the restrictive nature of teaching in schools means teachers need to be equipped with tools and attitudes that enable them to support independent development of beliefs, knowledge and mathematical thinking. Ernest (1989) suggests that confidence with regard to teaching mathematics will impact on teachers' knowledge via the perceived adequacy of that knowledge, recognising that attitudes to mathematics may affect attitudes to teaching mathematics, which then impacts on the classroom ethos. An enthusiastic teacher who continually demonstrates passion for the subject by 'doing mathematics' and talking about it in a positive way will generate an atmosphere where learners look forward to lessons as they enjoy the inquisitive nature of the subject, so developing the concept of being a mathematician. On the other hand, a less enthusiastic teacher may contribute to learners developing negative attitudes towards the subject.

REFLECTIVE QUESTIONS

What different views do teachers hold about teaching mathematics? What impact do these have in the classroom?

Developing subject knowledge

Shulman (1986), questioning how content and pedagogy are distinctive in the process of teaching, noted that 'mere content knowledge is likely to be as useless pedagogically as content-free skill' p8). This appears to be particularly relevant to the teaching of mathematics, given a disconnect between knowledge and transmission, which Campton and Stephenson (2014) conceive as a gap n 'the bridge between the teacher's knowledge and enabling students to know it' (p14). Shulman 1986) considers how a teacher prepares to teach something they have not found difficult, terming this 'learning for teaching' (p8). This is a skill that student teachers find very difficult to develop. Appropriate choice of examples is of paramount importance so that misconceptions are not created by the teacher. Beginning teachers sometimes cannot understand why learners are finding a topic difficult, or why consistent misconceptions arise, when these are due to the teacher's use of poor examples. In a mathematics lesson, low-attaining 16-year-olds were revising how to find the circumference and area of the circle. The student teacher taught just one example using a circle of radius 2 cm, resulting in a circumference of 4π cm and an area of 4π cm². So what happened next? The learners found the circumference for each question set and used the same solution to give the area of each circle. So, when the radius was 3 cm, the learners found the circumference to be 6π cm and then assumed the area was 6π cm². The student teacher was at a loss to understand why this was happening as they had not made the connection between learners' lack of understanding and he use of a 'poor example'. Mathematics teachers must be wary of creating misconceptions when teaching; they must be able to represent and formulate comprehensible subject matter by effective strategies to make mathematics accessible to learners and also to consider where misconceptions can be used as a teaching aid for understanding. It is for this reason that mathematics teachers must always work through the questions they set their learners when planning lessons so that they can anticipate the errors and/or misconceptions that may arise in the classroom. They must be prepared for the types of questions that will arise and occur during the lesson and view the lesson from the perspective of the learner.

McNamara (1991) echoes the idea that good mathematics teachers need an armoury of examples, explanations, demonstrations and illustrations to make subject matter knowledge comprehensible to learners. Shulman's (1986) notion of content knowledge suggests that teachers must be aware of he curriculum and associated materials, such as specifications and examinations, referring to these programmes as teachers' 'tools of the trade' (Shulman, 1987, p8). These, along with good teaching materials, provide support for beginning teachers in developing the 'right kind' of subject knowledge.

Ball et al. (2008) describe horizon content knowledge as 'knowledge beyond that being taught to students' (p400), developed from earlier work by Ball (1990), who defined horizon knowledge as awareness of how topics are related throughout the curriculum. Ma (2010) suggests that teachers can only learn about the grade (or year group) they teach by actually teaching it, but they also need to be aware of both the preceding grade and the next grade. All good teachers of mathematics must know mathematics prior to and beyond the content of what they teach.

Watson (2008) suggests that mathematical knowledge is active, as it develops by 'doing mathematics and being mathematical' (p3). A mathematics teacher must be mathematical, by working through the questions given to learners so that difficulties learners may encounter are anticipated well in advance, but also by displaying their love and enthusiasm for the subject by engaging with mathematical puzzles and perhaps having a 'mathematics for pleasure' reading section on display in their classroom. Transferring 'love' for the subject to learners is an essential skill that mathematics teachers must hold.

CHAPTER SUMMARY

Key points covered in this chapter are:

- the types of understanding of mathematics needed by teachers;
- the importance of good content knowledge for teachers;
- the impact of teachers' beliefs about mathematics;
- some of the ways that teachers can develop their content knowledge in mathematics.

Further reading

Donaldson, G., Field, J., Harries, D., Tope, C. and Taylor, H. (2012) *Becoming a Primary Mathematics Specialist Teacher*. Abingdon: Routledge.

This book provides an accessible guide to the role of a primary mathematics specialist. Although written for the previous curriculum, the content is highly relevant to today's teachers. Key literature is cited along with further reading. The chapters on deep subject knowledge and pedagogical knowledge particularly support primary subject leaders.

Southall, E. (2017) *Yes, but Why? Teaching for Understanding in Mathematics*. London: SAGE.

Ed Southall's book aims to help beginning teachers of mathematics in particular to see connections in mathematics and to see how 'maths makes sense' by exploring some of the understanding behind topics in the secondary school mathematics curriculum.

References

Alcock, L. (2017) *Mathematics Rebooted: A Fresh Approach to Understanding*. Oxford: Oxford University Press.

Askew, M., Brown, M., Rhodes, V., Johnson, D. and Wiliam, D. (1997) *Effective Teachers of Numeracy*. London: King's College.

Ball, D. (1990) 'The mathematical understandings that prospective teachers bring to teacher education'. *Elementary School Journal*, 90: 449–66.

Ball, D., Thames, M. and Phelps, G. (2008) 'Content knowledge for teaching: what makes it special?'. *Journal of Teacher Education*, 59(5): 389–407.

Beswick, K. (2012) 'Teachers beliefs about school mathematics and mathematicians' mathematics and their relationship to practice'. *Educational Studies in Mathematics*, 79(1): 127–47.

Beswick, K., Callingham, R. and Watson, J. (2012) 'The nature and development of middle school mathematics teachers' knowledge'. *Journal of Mathematics Teacher Education*, 15(2): 131–57.

Borko, H., Eisenhart, M., Brown, C., Underhill, R., Jones, D. and Agard, P. (1992) 'Learning to teach hard mathematics: do novice teachers and their instructors give up too easily?' *Journal for Research in Mathematics Education*, 23(3): 194–222.

Boylan, M., Maxwell, B., Wolstenholme, C. and Jay, T. (2017) *Longitudinal Evaluation of the Mathematics Teacher Exchange: China–England – Third Interim Report*. London: DfE.

Boylan, M., Maxwell, B., Wolstenholme, C., Jay, T. and Demack, S. (2018) 'The mathematics teacher exchange and "mastery" in England: the evidence for the efficacy of component practices'. *Education Sciences*, 8(4): 202.

Boylan, M., Wolstenholme, C., Demack, S., Maxwell, B., Jay, T., Adams, G. and Reaney, S. (2019) *Longitudinal Evaluation of the Mathematics Teacher Exchange: China–England – Final Report*. London: DfE.

Bruner, J. (1966) *Toward a Theory of Instruction*. Cambridge, MA: Harvard University Press.

Campton, I. and Stephenson, M. (2014) 'Partnering theory and practice in mathematics teaching'. In R. Hyde and J.-A. Edwards (eds), *Mentoring Mathematics Teachers: Supporting and Inspiring Pre-Service and Newly Qualified Teachers*. Abingdon: Routledge, pp7–24.

Chen, X. and Li, Y. (2010) 'Instructional coherence in Chinese mathematics classrooms: a case study on lessons in fraction division'. *International Journal of Science and Mathematics Education*, 8: 711–35.

Department for Education (DfE) (2014) *National Curriculum in England: Mathematics Programmes of Study*. Available at: www.gov.uk/government/publications/national-curriculum-in-england-mathematics-programmes-of-study/national-curriculum-in-england-mathematics-programmes-of-study

Ding, M., Li, Y., Li, X. and Gu, J. (2013) 'Knowing and understanding instructional mathematics content through intensive studies of textbooks'. In Y. Li and R. Huang (eds), *How Chinese Teach Mathematics and Improve Teaching*. New York: Routledge, pp66–82.

Edwards, R., Hyde, R., O'Connor, M. and Oldham, J. (2015) 'The importance of subject knowledge for mathematics teaching: an analysis of feedback from subject knowledge enhancement courses'. In G. Adams (ed.), *Proceedings of the British Society for Research into Learning Mathematics*, 35(3): 37–42.

Ernest, P. (1989) 'The knowledge, beliefs and attitudes of the mathematics teacher: a model'. *Journal of Education for Teaching*, 15(1): 13–33.

Fujita, T. and Hyde, R. (2014) 'Approaches to learning mathematics'. In R. Hyde and J.-A. Edwards (eds), *Mentoring Mathematics Teachers: Supporting and Inspiring Pre-Service and Newly Qualified Teachers*. Abingdon: Routledge, pp42–58.

Henderson, P., Hodgen, J., Foster, C. and Kuchemann, D. (2017) *Improving Mathematics in Key Stages 2 and 3: Guidance Report*. London: EEF.

Holm, J. and Kajander, A. (2012) 'Interconnections of knowledge and beliefs in teaching mathematics'. *Canadian Journal of Science, Mathematics and Technology Education*, 12(1): 7–21.

Kagan, S. (1992) 'Professional growth among preservice and beginning teachers'. *Review of Educational Research*, 62(2): 129–69.

Leong, Y.H., Ho, W.K. and Cheng, L.P. (2015) 'Concrete–pictorial–abstract: surveying its origins and charting its future'. *The Mathematics Educator*, 16(1): 1–18.

Ma, L. (2010) *Knowing and Teaching Elementary Mathematics: Teachers' Understanding of Fundamental Mathematics in China and the United States*, 2nd edn. New York: Routledge.

McNamara, D. (1991) 'Subject knowledge and its application: problems and possibilities for teacher educators'. *Journal of Education for Teaching*, 17(2): 113–28.

National Centre for Excellence in the Teaching of Mathematics (NCETM) (2017) *Five Big Ideas in Teaching for Mastery*. Available at: www.ncetm.org.uk/resources/50042

National Centre for Excellence in the Teaching of Mathematics (NCETM) (2019) *Secondary Mastery Professional Development Materials*. Available at: www.ncetm.org.uk/resources/53449

Needham, L. (2018) 'Using concrete manipulatives to re-engage disaffected learners in maths'. *Equals*, 23(2): 3–7.

Shao, G., Huang, R., Ding, E. and Li, Y. (2013) 'Mathematics classroom instruction viewed from a historical perspective'. In Y. Li and R. Huang (eds), *How Chinese Teach Mathematics and Improve Teaching*. New York: Routledge, pp11–28.

Schoenfeld, A. (1994) 'Doing and teaching mathematics'. In A. Schoenfeld (ed.), *Mathematical Thinking and Problem Solving*. Hillsdale, NJ: Lawrence Erlbaum Associates.

Shulman, L. (1986) 'Those who understand: knowledge growth in teaching'. *Educational Researcher*, 15(2): 4–14.

Shulman, L. (1987) 'Knowledge and teaching: foundations of the new reform'. *Harvard Educational Review*, 57(1): 1–21.

Thompson, A. (1992) 'Teachers' beliefs and conceptions: a synthesis of the research'. In A. Grouws (ed.), *Handbook of Research on Mathematics Learning and Teaching*. New York: Macmillan, pp127–46.

Watson, A. (2008) 'School mathematics as a special kind of mathematics'. *For the Learning of Mathematics*, 28(3): 3–7.

Watson, A. and Mason, J. (2006) 'Seeing an exercise as a single mathematical object: using variation to structure sense-making'. *Mathematics Thinking and Learning*, 8(2): 91–111.

Zhang, Q. and Wong, N.-Y. (2015) 'Beliefs, knowledge and teaching: a series of studies about Chinese mathematics teachers'. In L. Fan, N.-Y. Wong, J. Cai and S. Li (eds), *How Chinese Teach Mathematics: Perspectives from Insiders*. Singapore: World Scientific Publishing, pp457–92.

6

LEARNING FROM OTHER WORLDS

PINKY JAIN

KEYWORDS: CONSISTENCY; CULTURE-SPECIFIC PEDAGOGIES; CURRICULUM DESIGN; PROGRESSION; SHANGHAI MATHEMATICS; TEACHER SUBJECT KNOWLEDGE; TEACHER EDUCATION

CHAPTER OBJECTIVES

This chapter will allow you to achieve the following outcomes:

- explore the key features of the education systems in a range of countries identified through international measures as having outcomes for mathematics that are higher than England;
- consider the key pedagogical features of teaching in each country in relation to deep understanding of mathematics;
- consider the structural features of each country that support mathematics teaching;
- distil key lessons that can be learnt from each country and how they might provide support in developing the best approaches to teaching mathematics.

Introduction

One of the most effective ways to learn about oneself is by taking seriously the cultures of others. It forces you to pay attention to those details of life which differentiate them from you.

(Hall, 1959, p21)

In this chapter, I will be exploring a range of countries where mathematics teaching has a different approach to England. The idea is to explore each country from a cultural, societal and educational perspective to consider the curriculum, as well as teachers' experiences and backgrounds. By looking at different approaches, we should learn more about how mathematics might be taught better in England and also what might not be the best approach for us given the background and cultural context of each country. Though learning and how the brain assimilates knowledge are the same physiologically in all humans, there are a plethora of other factors that come into play when looking at the teaching and learning processes. It would be naive to assume that we can pick up ideas from one cultural context and implement them in our own.

The chapter considers four countries – China (Shanghai), Singapore, Switzerland and Canada – in order to understand and develop ideas that will improve practice within schools and individual classrooms to enable deep conceptual understanding of mathematics (mastery). This will not be a detailed review of each country, but will use a broad brushstroke to understand the structural differences between them and England in order to help us enhance our ways of working to teach mathematics. Furthermore, understanding the cultural narrative that is present in mathematics teaching, curriculum development and investment in teachers will support the development of ideas that can be learnt from other jurisdictions.

REFLECTIVE QUESTION

What is the role of wider cultural issues in ensuring that outcomes for mathematics are high for all children?

The whole wide world

Mathematics as a subject is unique in its nature as every population, cultural group and country engages in the use of informal or formal mathematics. It forms part of the fabric of all societies. This commonality presents a unique opportunity to compare, explore and develop a deep understanding of a range of different approaches, and the impact of these approaches on learners' mathematics. However, it does pose some challenges given that there are many choices and variations to consider. To select countries that might help us to improve our way of teaching, or even just confirm that our choices are right, we have used the Trends in International Mathematics and Science Study (TIMSS) 2015 (Mullis et al., 2016) and Programme for International Student Assessment (PISA) 2015 (OECD, 2016b) test rankings. Though there are some flaws, and many have criticised the design and even the use of TIMSS and PISA tests, they provide us with some comparisons that support the selection of countries which might be worth exploring. We are going to explore countries that have achieved more highly than England as well as countries that are culturally similar. The countries under consideration are China (Shanghai), Singapore, Switzerland and Canada, with Switzerland and Canada being much closer in cultural and societal structure than Shanghai and Singapore. For each country, we will look at the state school system, the cultural background in relation to educational values, the structure of teacher education and working patterns in school, the curriculum, and key pedagogical features worthy of note. There is no suggestion that using countries which have higher scores in a few tests means that English education is somehow inferior; it is merely a way of selecting countries for focus. Much importance has been given by the English government on the outcomes of these tests, and our relatively poor performance has meant that there has been significant financial investment to increase England's rankings. This investment in learning from high-performing jurisdictions is of great value if we recognise that there are many nuances which must be accepted when considering how different countries work. A simple copy-and-paste approach will not lead to similar outcomes.

China (Shanghai)

The schooling structure in Shanghai is similar to that in England, with state schools offering early childhood education up to the age of 6 before learners move on to primary for the next six years and then lower secondary for another three years. There is an interesting difference in the selection of students for upper secondary education within the Shanghai system. Learners are streamed depending upon their performance in the entrance exams into academic or vocational paths. There are parallel private systems in place as there are in the UK. The educational culture can be encapsulated by the words 'knowledge transmission' (Tan, 2012, p156). The focus is on instruction through a centralised system that is carefully considered, systematic and well-funded. There is a National Curriculum with high-stakes examinations that stream students according to their outcomes. The curriculum design has good constructive alignment between the content, assessment and teaching. There seems to be a countrywide view that education is to be highly regarded, a commitment to meritocracy, and that social cohesion through education – with strong state and citizen support – is the key to developing and maintaining a highly civilised society. The educational culture within Shanghai is 'top-down', with national bodies undertaking tasks such as prescribing textbooks. Modes of teaching, at first sight, are very procedural and teacher-led, with lots of drill and practice. There is great emphasis on the correct representation and procedures for performing calculations. Furthermore, there is emphasis on knowledge transmission and then practice to ensure that knowledge has been retained and can be applied. This means that teachers take great care and a good deal of time when planning and constructing the mathematics for a lesson to ensure that it is purposefully and carefully considered. In comparison with England, there is more emphasis on a concrete–pictorial–abstract (CPA) approach in the way that mathematics is presented, and though there appears to be greater teacher talk, we must look deeper into the lesson structure as well as the school structure. Boylan et al. (2019) have carried out an evaluation of the Shanghai Mathematics Teacher Exchange (a UK government-funded programme where teachers from Shanghai came to England, and vice versa). There is evidence from this report that 'Shanghai whole-class interactive teaching aims to develop conceptual understanding and procedural fluency. This is achieved through lessons designed to be accessible to all, through skilful use of teacher questioning and incremental progression' (Boylan et al., 2019, p26).

This may suggest that lessons are very teacher-led, which does not sit well with our culture of a child-oriented constructivist approach, and raises questions about the depth of understanding and transferability of knowledge. However, what we find is:

Teaching is supported by well-crafted mathematical models and exemplar problems, as well as practice materials that focus on critical aspects of mathematical learning. To ensure pupils progress together, tasks are designed to allow for extension by deepening understanding of concepts and proce-dures, and daily intervention is used to support those needing extra tuition.

(Boylan et al., 2019, p26)

Learner talk is a key priority, although it is teacher-directed and structured differently in primary and secondary schools. Furthermore, 'curricula progression, lesson timing, and teacher roles and responsibilities are organised at a school level to support these approaches to mathematics teaching and learning' (Boylan et al., 2019, p26).

In Shanghai, all learners are taught by specialist teachers in mathematics. This is not the case in England, where generalist teachers teach all learners across the primary school, and at times – due to the shortage of mathematics teachers – at secondary too. This is coupled with Shanghai teachers spending ten times more time on professional development than English teachers (40 days versus 4 days) (Sellen, 2016, p34). Furthermore, Shanghai teachers spend 18 per cent less time in school than English teachers and also spend more time on activities such as planning, marking, teamwork, pastoral care and school management, as well as more time with parents, than in England, but less on general administration and extracurricular activities (OECD, 2016a). Shanghai teachers also only teach one or two lessons a day to the whole class, with the remaining time spent on remedial lessons.

The distribution of time for Shanghai teachers is vastly different to that in England. Co-planning and the provision of more purposeful feedback and assessment of learning to support the next steps is a vital key to student outcomes. The organisation of schools such that learners have the same teachers for mathematics for three or more years seems to be having a positive impact on outcomes.

The final pieces of the puzzle that go some way to explaining the lower ranking of England com-pared with Shanghai are the cultural beliefs and societal attitudes about education. The approach that all learners can achieve highly and the expectation that learners carry out independent study are key features of Shanghai teaching. Boylan et al. (2019) identify that a high level of parental involvement in their children's education through support and provision of resources plays a role in the high outcomes in mathematics.

In summary, though the overall structure of schooling and the curriculum are similar between England and Shanghai, there is careful and purposeful use of resources to ensure that progress is made with every investment. Interestingly, Boylan et al. (2019) comment:

Primary mathematics lessons in England have been marked by low levels of interaction between teacher and pupils, including during whole-class episodes. The format that has dominated has been teacher explanation in a transmissive manner, followed by individual practice or group practice. Practice has tended to be based on worksheets or other resources that focus on routine problems and use of textbooks has been rare.

(p37)

In England, the emphasis has been on ensuring that there is a degree of differentiation, with the focus being on the learner's ability as opposed to the mathematical concept being covered.

There are many more subtle differences between the two systems that could be considered. However, for the purposes of our understanding of the practices that have the greatest impact on the learning of mathematics, the greatest difference is in the approach and understanding of learners, in that within Shanghai, the philosophical attitude seems to be that all children can learn if we as teachers can structure their learning and teach with the approach that learning can take place. Also, the cultural beliefs within the whole society that everyone can do mathematics have an essential role to play in the success of Shanghai learners in mathematics. Within England, we approach learning from the child's perspective, and there is 'a pervasive belief that mathematical ability is fixed and leads to differentiated access to the curriculum' (Boylan et al., 2019, p38), as well as a diluting of ideas to suit learners who may not have understood the concepts.

The key features of the Shanghai approach can be summarised into three themes: investment into teaching, training structures, and cultural beliefs about the ability of learners to do mathematics.

Singapore

The Singapore system of education is broadly similar to England, with children starting preschool from the age of 3. Compulsory primary school starts at the age of 6, then on to secondary school and to university, where students have the option to take part in pre-university courses. There are many different types of schools and pathways to gaining qualifications. Schooling is free in the state system, though there are also private schools. The Ministry of Education (MoE) states as its intent that every Singaporean must complete their formal education. There is a common purpose to the education system, which has been identified as a child having:

> *a good sense of self-awareness, a sound moral compass, and the necessary skills and knowledge to take on challenges of the future. He is responsible to his family, community and nation. He appreciates the beauty of the world around him, possesses a healthy mind and body, and has a zest for life.*

> (MoE, 2009)

This is really an interesting perspective and gives great clarity to how schools may make their choices and the outcomes that are expected. The curriculum is planned with three key facets: subject-based knowledge, skills through subject, and character development.

> *The broad aims of mathematics education in Singapore are to enable students to:*

> * *acquire and apply mathematical concepts and skills;*

> * *develop cognitive and metacognitive skills through a mathematical approach to problem solving; and*

> * *develop positive attitudes towards mathematics.*

> (MoE, 2012, p7)

These are very different to the three aims of the English National Curriculum, which do not consider the role of learning disposition in supporting the development of mathematical understanding. The Singaporean curriculum is similar to ours in that there is a slow building of ideas and connections made throughout the content. There is explicit emphasis within the curriculum to remind teachers 'to have the big picture in the mind so that they can better understand the role of each syllabus, the connection it makes with the next level' (MoE, 2012, p11).

There is a greater emphasis on problem-solving and consideration of what this means in its broadest sense. The view that problem-solving is the lynchpin of all aspects of mathematical outcomes that Singaporean teachers should be aiming for is the central doctrine of the curriculum. The content is less cluttered and more focused on building foundational skills in primary that lead up to more complex skills in secondary. This is centrally supported by Prime Minister Lee Hsien Loong (2004): 'We've got to teach less to our students so that they will learn more' (p24).

There are exemplifications of the learning experience as part of the curriculum content that are shared with teachers. Also, the curriculum design recognises wider elements such as attitudes that impact on the learning.

In Singapore, teachers spend similar total hours in school compared to English teachers but teach for 16 per cent fewer hours. However, as with Shanghai teachers, the distribution of their time is managed very differently to that of English teachers, with more emphasis on extracurricular, planning, marking and student counselling, with teachers receiving three times as many days on professional development activities compared to English teachers (OECD, 2016a). With investment in educational research increasing by 132 per cent from 48 million Singapore dollars in 2002–2007 to 111.58 million Singapore dollars in 2013–2017 (Kwek, 2018), the system is centralised as in England and Shanghai, with funding, syllabus and exams all being managed through a top-down approach. The MoE also manages the allocation of teachers to schools, as well as the hiring and firing of teachers. All teachers are expected to have postgraduate qualifications, with the structure of training and the curriculum being similar to that of a British Postgraduate Certificate in Education (PGCE), but lasting 16 months, with teachers being paid to train. When looking at the overall structure and philosophy of the Singapore system, what is striking is the level of connectivity in the structure of the education system to support the educational doctrine that they have established, with the key premise embedded throughout, being that all children can achieve, as well as 'Belief. It's one of the most important lessons a teacher can teach. One that can begin a powerful change in a child's life' (MoE, 2019). This is a powerful statement, and one that really defines the cultural perspective of the Singapore education system.

Culturally, there are key societal features that are very different to England. There is a strong social imperative to ensure all children have a successful start, and the government has demonstrated this through increased investment in education. The mathematics classroom is a manifestation of this cultural expectation that all individuals can achieve given the right support and effort, with greater emphasis being on learner attributes and much less on procedural efficiency. Schleicher says, 'Mathematics in Singapore is not about knowing everything. It's about thinking like a mathematician' (cited in Vasagar, 2016).

This is a key fundamental difference in the way that mathematics teaching is approached in Singapore compared to England. They maintain a whole-class approach, with key questions to all children to think and problem-solve. Gaps are addressed with speed and the process is very industrialised. One of the main challenges to this way of teaching and learning is the reduction in the level of creativity given that the emphasis is on achieving high grades. This drive to achieve comes from a deep-rooted anxiety in Singaporean children of 'being afraid to lose out', or 'kiasu' (Vasagar, 2016).

Having examined two countries, the two key ideas emerging that have an impact upon mathematics achievement are those of curriculum content and educational philosophy, including the extent to which this is embedded within the societal systems and the degree of alignment between all the educational structures. With both Shanghai and Singapore, the philosophy is connected to cultural and societal beliefs, and is manifested with clarity in the education systems and political decision-making. This synergistic approach allows all within the system to focus efforts in the same direction. In both Singapore and Shanghai, the curriculum content for mathematics is far less and there is greater time spent on each idea, so there is deeper coverage, and not the shallow, hasty look we might experience in England.

We now continue the examination with countries that might be deemed closer not only geographically, but also culturally, and see why they are ranked above England.

Switzerland

Switzerland is ranked 8th for mathematics scores in the PISA 2015 tables (OECD, 2016a), but there are no scores for Switzerland in the TIMSS tables as they did not participate, which is in itself interesting. The system of education is broadly similar to England, with children going to school for 11 years and completing compulsory education. Around 95 per cent of children go to a state school. One of the unique features of the Swiss system is that there are a range of paths that children can take, from training programmes to traditional academic routes. Children move fluidly from one system to another as and when they make their choices. The system is open and operates flexibly. The Swiss system has above-average attainment in mathematics among OECD countries, and this has been stable over the years. Unlike Singapore and Shanghai, the Swiss system is entirely decentralised and schools are managed by cantons. There is a different system in each canton, even down to the starting age of children in school, which varies from 4 to 6 years old. The school day, structure of schools, and languages are also very different in each canton; however, state education is free across all of Switzerland. With such a complex range of variables, it is challenging to see why and how Switzerland is still able to rank above England. One of the key differences between Switzerland and the other countries under consideration is in the parity with which vocational (technical) education is treated and funded against academic courses, and the fluidity with which these two options work together. The support learners receive is not to compensate for failure, but to ensure that failure does not occur, through positive options for each learner and the placement of learners on the most appropriate pathway for them.

Within Switzerland, time is provided within the working day or week for teachers to engage in professional development activities to develop the skills needed in order to address the challenges and issues they face. There is emphasis on peer-to-peer collaboration, with time given at all stages to support teachers to develop in areas where they need individual support. The training of teachers is carried out in universities dedicated to teacher education, not generalist universities. As in England, not all primary teachers are mathematics specialists and there is a mixture of specialisms in secondary. In this respect, there is close alignment to the system in England. One of the unique features of the Swiss system is that in some cantons, learners who do not do well are kept in the same year group and do not progress to the next year group; however, there is no stigma. The range of options means that learners are able to work to their strengths and there is no one-size-fits-all approach.

The societal view of education is that it is an equal shared responsibility between parents and teachers. The school day gives a good example of this, whereby lunch is mainly had at home or in non-school communal settings. Schools are closed for one day or afternoon a week, allowing teachers time to engage in other activities. This very local approach to the management of education through the 26 cantons creates a very diverse and culturally rich experience in Switzerland. There are many different pedagogical approaches, and these allow learners to gain good outcomes.

There has been some debate as to whether this individual regional diversity might have a negative impact on the system. In recent years, there have been moves to unify the canton educational approaches so that resources can support and ensure some continuity across all cantons. Though the factors considered here for Switzerland are not the same as Shanghai or Singapore, or with the same data set – as the availability of centralised data is limited – the factors that are having an impact on outcomes are similar: investment in teaching, training structures (high level of subject knowledge), cultural values of education, a clear educational philosophy, curriculum design, and choice.

The Swiss belief that *la Suisse n'existe pas* (Switzerland does not exist) (Milošević, 2016) encapsulates the non-uniformity and diversity seen within such a small geographical space.

There is a real sense in the research around the Swiss education system of ensuring that all learners are engaged and work well. Teacher knowledge in mathematics is of a very high level (Ingvarson et al., 2013) and great responsibility is given to teachers to make pedagogical choices to suit their learners.

Due to its population size, Switzerland benefits from small class sizes, though Hattie (2008) argues that this is not an influencing factor. However, when coupled with high levels of teacher subject knowledge (which is formally examined in teacher training programmes), this could be key to high performance in Switzerland.

REFLECTIVE QUESTION

This chapter identifies investment in teaching, training structures (high level of subject knowledge), cultural values of education, a clear educational philosophy, curriculum design, and choice as key factors in the success of education systems in Shanghai, Singapore and Switzerland. To what extent are these present in England?

Canada

The last country we will look at is Canada, one of our closest relations and one where there has been historical influence and legacy left from England.

Canada, like Switzerland, does not have a centralised system for education. Individual provinces and territories are in control of how education is structured. This leads to a range of schools and a large number of variables in how schools are run and managed. Though there is variety and a complex approach to education, the OECD's education director, Andreas Schleicher, has observed that the 'big uniting theme is equity' (cited in Coughlan, 2017). The common push for an equal chance to learn and develop all children has been the binding factor in Canada's educational progress.

Teachers in Canada (we have considered Alberta as it is most closely culturally aligned to England) spend 3 per cent more time in school than English teachers. However, again, the distribution of their time is very different to England, with more time given to pastoral care, teaching and extra-curricular activities, and less time given to marking, planning and administration, with the overall focus being on teaching and learning activities and the autonomy that teachers have in the lesson (OECD, 2016a). The mathematics programme of studies in Alberta starts with establishing with its teachers an understanding that belief about students and mathematics learning is key to success in student outcomes: 'The learning environment should value and respect the diversity of students' experiences and ways of thinking' (Alberta Education, 2016, p1).

This positive attitude is an important aspect of an effective outcome. The Canadian focus on learner disposition and how they may approach and value mathematics is not so different to the Singaporean philosophy of belief. The cultural value of inclusive practice, which aims for outcomes to be the same for all children, can be seen through Alberta's curriculum documentation. Though it is not absolutely clear that this will be the same across all aspects of the Canadian population, it is a fairly typical representation from which we can extrapolate that this is the general attitude towards the learning of mathematics.

When we couple this inclusive approach, where all students are seen as having the potential to succeed, with the investment and support given to teachers in developing their own skills, it is not surprising that children's outcomes have a positive impact.

In Alberta, the mathematical content is comparable to that of England, but the programme of study presents this in an interesting manner. There is greater emphasis on supporting learners to think mathematically and make connections within the mathematics, with problem-solving, reasoning, visualisation and talk as key pedagogical points that form part of the direction given to teachers. This top-down philosophical approach to mathematics, as well as its place in school and the wider community, with the belief that everyone can do mathematics, is a key way that the curriculum encourages teachers to teach fewer concepts and spend more time exploring ideas. The spiral nature of the curriculum means that concepts are visited at different points in a learner's time through school. There is an emphasis on an enquiry-based approach that not all within the system are appreciative of, though there is a strong group of teachers who feel that the approach allows for individualisation of mathematics, allows children to construct understanding, and has long-term benefits. Overall, Canada has taken a structured approach to address a key objective for its society – that of inclusive outcomes for all children in mathematics.

There is a clear strategy in Canada to only recruit high-performing teachers and support them to develop and stay in their careers (SCOPE, 2016). With no national ministry for education, each region is allowed to address the needs of its population, with places in teacher education programmes being very competitive in all regions. There is a high degree of training and expectation on those who choose to become teachers. There is no acceptance of individuals onto these programmes without high academic credentials. There is also a requirement in many provinces for primary teachers to complete a subject specialism that supports the high level of knowledge which ensures children are supported. All professional development is linked to individual growth plans and assessed against the teaching standards at an informal level. There is support for school-based research and funding for teachers to undertake personal projects, although the support available has reduced in the past few years. The impact of thinking and teaching in a research-informed manner will be long-lasting.

One of the pivotal aspects that has had an impact upon outcomes has been the approach to school improvement, which firmly believes that at all levels, there is a deep desire to improve and make individuals accountable, leading to a high level of teacher trust. SCOPE (2016) says, 'The approach to school improvement is not one of standardization of top-down directives … When we're working with boards or schools or teachers, it's a treasure hunt, not a witch hunt' (p7).

There is a very integrated structure for training and development at all stages of a teacher's career with teacher-directed professional learning. These programmes have had some significant outcomes, with 94 per cent of teachers reporting improvement in their knowledge and skills (SCOPE, 2016, p8). The philosophical belief is expressed by SCOPE (2016): 'by placing teachers at the center of the education system, preparing them well, and providing substantial support to them throughout their careers, Alberta has moved to the head of the educational pack' (p11).

Discussion and comparison

Having considered four countries, all different but similar in many ways, what are the lessons learnt with regard to the teaching of mathematics in English schools? The most striking theme to come from this brief analysis is that though the four countries are all different in their cultural approaches to teaching mathematics, there is a very strong embedded belief in each country that 'everyone can do mathematics'. This belief permeates in all aspects of the curriculum, teaching, support for teachers, and the structuring of the system. The design of all the curricula have the expectation that teachers will teach in a way that, if taught with care and supported, everyone can learn mathematics. The level of differentiation that we see within England, which to a great extent widens the gaps in learners' attainment, may be something that we should revisit. When looking at the structure of teaching, we do not see a lack of appreciation that children are all at different levels, but that there needs to be a strong onus on the teaching to ensure that all learners are supported to achieve the same outcomes. So, the lesson aim or objective is the same for all learners and the ways in which the educative experiences are established is to enable all learners to achieve at the same level. There is appreciation that abilities might be different but that all learners can achieve. This starting point really changes the way that we approach teaching because it is not a deficit model. Within England, most teachers would agree with this view, but we must consider whether our systems and governments feel this too.

The next theme to emerge is that of educational philosophy. Each country has a clear philosophical reason for the purpose of education within society, with a shared vision as to why learners go to school. All four of the countries examined have a different philosophical standing, but nonetheless they have a standpoint that is aligned with the society in which education takes place and is operationalised at all levels of the education system. Having clear, agreed principles for education empowers all decisions that are made to be aligned.

As the four countries have culturally different heritages, it would be naive to lift the structure, approach or even just the curriculum from these countries and import them to England. This would just not work as it relies on the two fundamental values that we have just mentioned – a shared belief system and a clear educational philosophy. However, we can – at local level – operationalise this approach to education by having an agreed belief and joint school philosophy. What are your beliefs about mathematics as a school? Are these the same as your parents' beliefs? What are your values and principles about the purpose of mathematics education as a school? If you can agree on these as a whole school, it will support in developing constructive alignment for the delivery of mathematics.

The next theme identified in this review is the considerable level of investment in teacher education and support in the development of high levels of teacher subject knowledge. All four countries invested more than England in professional development as well as days given to teachers to learn outside the classroom and consider self-directed development, with the highest-performing countries giving the most time. This should give us a clear steer that supporting and encouraging teachers to recognise their strengths, as well as giving opportunities to develop areas, results in better student outcomes.

We must consider how time is spent by teachers in school and ask if we spend a disproportionate amount of time on a range of activities that have the lowest impact on learners' outcomes, such as administration. This is an indication of another theme, that of trust in teachers. All four systems depend upon schools and teachers being autonomous in order to decide how teaching takes place. The approach of the governing systems must be that of understanding that teachers are able to do their job and supporting them to do so. There is no mechanism of inspection in any of these countries and their systems are allowed to improve themselves. We do not have control over the top-down approach or the lack of trust the government has in teachers in England, but at the local level we can structure our departments and schools to ensure that there is a culture of support, not a deficit model in which teachers are not trusted.

Another theme identified in this chapter is that of a deep-rooted approach which relies on collaboration between teachers and schools, and as a system to support improvement. All of the countries spent a greater proportion of their time than England on activities involving communicating with parents and also on student pastoral care. The data also indicate that the percentage of time spent on professional development (of the total allocated time which for England was the lowest in comparison to the four countries) which was linked to network development and collaborative research was higher in these four countries than in England. This gives us an opportunity to examine this at both the national and local level. What type of professional development should we be investing in to ensure development of mathematics teachers? It is clearly not just on the one-off continuous professional development (CPD) day, but more so on developing long-lasting approaches that allow teachers to work at their own pace to continually develop their teaching skills. This comes down to the choices we make as schools and the ways we allocate our very limited funding as leaders in our subject. Sometimes the best CPD is provided by the opportunity for teachers to get together in a group, consider ideas and share good practice. When this is layered with research-informed choices, it makes for outcomes that are more likely to have an impact on learning.

The final theme to emerge from this analysis is with regard to curriculum content. All the countries considered have chosen the pragmatic approach of not assuming that we need to cover all aspects of mathematics with all learners, but an approach that aims to develop learners to 'think like a mathematician'. The curricular aim focuses on understanding, making connections and problem-solving, which the English curriculum also focuses on, but in the four countries examined there is a narrower range of content to achieve the attitude at primary that is needed to ensure a positive risk-taking approach is achieved to support secondary development. There is a general consensus in all four countries that 'less is more' and that there is benefit in a slower movement through mathematics.

There is much more focus upon the understanding of mathematical concepts built on research carried out in the UK, such as Skemp's (1976) work. This approach relies upon strong teacher subject knowledge and ensuring that learning is broken down into many steps, with use of CPA, talk and problem-solving being key pedagogical tools.

CHAPTER SUMMARY

Key points covered in this chapter are:

- the education, cultural differences, curriculum differences, support for teachers, and investment into teacher professional development across four countries identifies six key themes;
- these six themes are: belief, central educational philosophy, strong teacher subject knowledge, trust for individual teachers, collaborative approach, and reduction in content with slowing down teaching;
- it is possible to adapt these themes into tools that can be used in English classrooms;
- these themes, even if implemented at the local level, will have an impact on children's learning and understanding, developing them as mathematicians.

Further reading

Crehan, L. (2016) *Cleverlands: The Secrets behind the Success of the World's Education Superpowers*. London: Unbound.

This book looks even more closely at a range of jurisdictions and unpicks what can be learnt from them.

Westover, T. (2018) *Educated: The International Bestselling Memoir*. London: Windmill Books.

In order to truly establish the principles for teaching mathematics, reading this publication will help consider things in an alternative perspective.

References

Alberta Education (2016) *Mathematics Kindergarten to Grade 9*. Available at: https://education.alberta.ca/media/3115252/2016_k_to_9_math_pos.pdf

Boylan, M., Wolstenholme, C., Demack, S., Maxwell, B., Jay, T., Adams, G. and Reaney, S. (2019) *Longitudinal Evaluation of the Mathematics Teacher Exchange: China–England – Final Report*. London: DfE.

Coughlan, S. (2017) How Canada Became an Education Superpower. *BBC News*, 2 August. Available at: www.bbc.co.uk/news/business-40708421

Hall, E.T. (1959) *The Silent Language*. New York: Doubleday.

Hattie, J. (2008) *Visible Learning: A Synthesis of Over 800 Meta-Analyses Relating to Achievement.* Abingdon: Routledge.

Ingvarson, L., Schwille, J., Tatto, M.T., Rowley, G., Peck, R. and Senk, S.L. (2013) *An Analysis of Teacher Education Context, Structure, and Quality-Assurance Arrangements in TEDS-M Countries.* Amsterdam: IEA.

Kwek, D. (2018) *Overview of the Education System and Education Research in Singapore.* Available at: http://yozma.mpage.co.il/SystemFiles/Overview%20Singapore.pdf

Loong, L.H. (2004) *Our Future of Opportunity and Promise.* Available at: http://ncee.org/wp-content/uploads/2017/01/Sgp-non-AV-3-PM-Lee-2004-Our-Future-of-Opportunity-and-Promise-Teach-Less-Learn-More.pdf

Milošević, Z. (2016) 'The customs and culture of Switzerland: the living tradition, a survived past'. *Diplomacy & Commerce*, 17 September. Available at: www.diplomacyandcommerce.rs/the-customs-and-culture-of-switzerland-the-living-tradition-a-survived-past/

Ministry of Education (MoE) (2009) *The Desired Outcomes of Education.* Available at: www.moe.gov.sg/docs/default-source/document/education/files/desired-outcomes-of-education.pdf

Ministry of Education (MoE) (2012) *Mathematics Syllabus Primary One to Six.* Available at: www.moe.gov.sg/docs/default-source/document/education/syllabuses/sciences/files/mathematics_syllabus_primary_1_to_6.pdf

Ministry of Education (MoE) (2019) *Teach.* Available at: www.moe.gov.sg/careers/teach

Mullis, I.V.S., Martin, M.O., Foy, P. and Hooper, M. (2016) *TIMSS 2015 International Results in Mathematics.* Available at: http://timssandpirls.bc.edu/timss2015/international-results/

Organisation for Economic Co-operation and Development (OECD) (2016a) *Education at a Glance 2016: OECD Indicators.* Paris: OECD.

Organisation for Economic Co-operation and Development (OECD) (2016b) *PISA 2015 Results (Volume I): Excellence and Equity in Education.* Paris: OECD.

Sellen, P. (2016) *Teacher Workload and Professional Development in England's Secondary Schools: Insights from TALIS.* London: Education Policy Institute.

Skemp, R.R. (1976) 'Relational understanding and instrumental understanding'. *Mathematics Teaching*, 77: 20–6.

Stanford Center for Opportunity Policy in Education (SCOPE) (2016) *Canada: Diversity and Decentralization.* Available at: http://ncee.org/wp-content/uploads/2017/02/CanadaCountryBrief.pdf

Tan, C. (2012) 'The culture of education policy-making: curriculum reform in Shanghai'. *Critical Studies in Education*, 53(2): 153–67.

Vasagar, J. (2016) 'Why Singapore's kids are so good at maths'. *Financial Times*, 22 July. Available at: www.ft.com/content/2e4c61f2-4ec8-11e6-8172-e39ecd3b86fc

7

MOVING TOWARDS CLASSROOMS THAT FOSTER DEEP CONCEPTUAL UNDERSTANDING AND REASONING

ROSA ARCHER AND SALLY BAMBER

KEYWORDS: DEEP UNDERSTANDING; RELATIONAL UNDERSTANDING; LESSON STUDY; REASONING; TRANSFORMATIVE TEACHER EDUCATION

CHAPTER OBJECTIVES

This chapter will allow you to achieve the following outcomes:

- reflect on how teacher enquiry can support professional development and transform practice;
- reflect on a range of pedagogical approaches that encourage learners to develop deep mathematical understanding.

Introduction

Common and substantial benefits for pupils are linked to CPD that is research-informed and rich in research-related processes ... Benefits for teachers from participating in research-rich CPD activities include improved knowledge of subjects and teaching and learning strategies, willingness to innovate and continue learning, improved confidence and skills in matching teaching and learning strategies with individual needs, and confidence in embedding strategies highlighted as high leverage by research in their day to day practice.

(Cordingley, 2015, p236)

Through their transformative power, research communities in school have the potential to provide a model for professional learning that translates research into practice, as well as giving practitioners a space within schools to participate in authentic professional learning opportunities (Cochran-Smith and Lytle, 2009; Darling-Hammond, 2017). This chapter will discuss how groups of practitioners undertaking research can (re)professionalise their work, gaining a sense of agency and control over the knowledge and practice that allow more learners to master mathematics (Darling-Hammond, 2017; Swan, 2005). The examples of collaborative teacher enquiry that are applied here have the potential to achieve all of these features of professional learning. We share two models in which participants are not concerned with establishing wide communities of researchers, but are focused on small-scale, collaborative research enquiries, whereby the enquiry is centred on the site of learning and where participants are focused on how learning is developed within their classrooms (Darling-Hammond, 2017). The key participants are teachers and student teachers working alongside university teacher educators and other participants who share the roles of practitioner and researcher within the enquiry (Cochran-Smith and Lytle, 2009).

Models of transformative teacher education

The following case studies offer models of collaborative enquiry that are inspired by models such as the Japanese lesson study research groups (e.g. see Radovic et al., 2014) and the models of teacher research groups used in Hong Kong, which is also influenced by Japanese lesson study and Swedish models of learning study (Marton et al., 2019). Each model shares the following characteristics that are influenced by the principles of transformative teacher education discussed by many authors – in particular, Darling-Hammond (2017), but also Cochran-Smith and Lytle (2009), Cordingley (2015), Marton et al. (2019), Swan and Burkhardt (2014) and Zeichner (2003):

- creating a culture of enquiry and respect for teacher knowledge;

- encouraging lesson design that is focused on learning specific curriculum content;

- developing and controlling the enquiry focus;

- connecting to teachers' collaborative work in professional learning communities that is intensive and sustained over time;

- informing using research the enquiry design and implementation;

- respecting everyone's contribution and engaging in critical professional dialogue; and

- scrutinising the impact of learning models within the lesson design is scrutinised in relation to learners' responses.

REFLECTIVE QUESTIONS

Reflect on this list of principles relative to your own professional learning opportunities. Are there any points that you would remove or add to this? What might be the barriers to achieving these principles?

The following case studies address two projects that have attempted to capture the potential positive impact of the teacher research groups and lesson study cycles. Both models have the potential to inform professional learning for both experienced and beginning teachers, working collaboratively. We focus on the teachers' involvement in and perception of mathematics pedagogy in the first and the teachers' perceptions of the professional cycle in the second.

The first is a collaborative project that uses multiple representations of number within a number theory unit for 10- and 11-year-olds (Years 5 and 6) in an English primary school, following the model shown in Figure 7.1.

Preparation		Professional learning session
Teachers and university tutors meet to agree the focus for the teacher research group (TRG). Research that informs the project is shared.		Participants learn about the focus for the TRG, the concepts, pedagogy, current practice and research that informs the learning. The session is interactive and models lesson activities and resources. Reading sources are shared.

Professional learning session	Planning small group teaching
Participants learn how to transfer the outcomes of their small group teaching to each class's context. They reflect on the place of the learning models used in the TRG within their schools. They discuss potential barriers and opportunities for enhancing learning. They identify the significance of these models for their own professional knowledge and for their practice. Participants plan further reading and identify the significance of the outcomes of this TRG for their own practice.	Participants use the models learnt in the first session to design a lesson so that they can interpret the impact of the learning models on the learners' knowledge and understanding. They work with experts to design the lesson.

Small group teaching
Participants teach the lesson. In some cases, one participant observes while the other teaches. All participants focus on noticing the impact of the lesson design on the pupils' learning. They record significant comments or photograph pupils' work.

Review of teaching and learning
Participants review the impact of the learning models on the pupils' learning. They discuss significant comments or photograph pupils' work. They reflect on how their choices seemed to influence the learning. Participants interrogate the relationships between the teacher, learners and the mathematics.

Figure 7.1   The teacher research group model used in the case study (adapted from Bamber, 2018)

RESEARCH

Lesson study

Lesson study is a research-based approach to the professional development of teachers' that originated in Japan (Stigler and Hiebert, 1999). When conducting a lesson study cycle, a group of teachers jointly plan a lesson, observe learners' responses to the lesson and conduct a review in a post-lesson discussion. The aim of the lesson study cycle is to answer a question or research a particular issue. The presence of a research question agreed by the lesson study team distinguishes a research lesson from a demonstration lesson. The aim of the lesson study lesson is in fact to research a particular approach to teaching and learning and analyse learners' responses to such an approach, in contrast to a demonstration lesson, which fosters imitation and does not question the approach used. In each lesson study cycle, a considerable amount of time is spent studying the chosen issue and how this fits within the mathematics curriculum. The studying of existing literature and analysis of the particular circumstances (in Japanese, this is referred to as *kyozai kenkyu*) feeds into a very detailed lesson plan, with particular attention paid to learners' expected responses. Analysis of learners' responses and findings from the lesson should be generalised beyond the immediate context in order to increase pedagogical understanding, not only for the benefit of the individual class or teacher, but also for the profession as a whole. The knowledgeable other (or *koshi* in Japanese) plays a very important role in a lesson study cycle. The knowledgeable other is an experienced teacher outside the immediate setting who has the role of translating the theory into practice and advising the lesson study team on how to continue their study. Usually, the *koshi* has the final say in the post-lesson discussion. In England, where lesson study is not as widely available as in Japan, it might be difficult to have access to a fully trained *koshi*, and some flexibility might be needed when organising a lesson study cycle (Baldry and Foster, 2019). For example, in the case study analysed here, the university teacher educator takes the role of the *koshi*. In Japan, most teachers – primary school teachers in particular – are very familiar with lesson study and might need very little practical advice on how to conduct a lesson study cycle. However, in different settings, where teachers are much less experienced, the *koshi* could guide the lesson study team through the practicalities of the experience, advising them on how to use the literature available (Baldry and Foster, 2019) and guiding them on further study.

The second project involves teachers and student teachers working on a lesson study cycle as part of the initial teacher education (ITE) programme in the North of England. This chapter reflects on how the application of research to practice within the lesson study experience has the potential to transform practice.

The project, carried out over several years, involves student teachers working on lesson study alongside more experienced teachers and university teacher educators. The level of involvement of the schools and classroom teachers varies. In most of the schools, the teachers' participation in the planning and teaching of the lessons is limited to observing and feeding back; most of the planning is carried out by the student teachers, with guidance from the university teacher educators, who also act as *koshis* during the post-lesson discussion. In some schools, however, the more experienced teachers taught the lessons and were active participants in the planning and post-lesson discussions. Several planning sessions, lessons and post-lesson discussions, as well as interviews with participants, were audio-recorded and analysed. Findings from this study have also been reported in Archer (2016) and Radovic et al. (2014).

In each case, research that informs mathematics teaching and learning is used within a collaborative community. Participants design the lessons and interrogate the impact of chosen representations, problems and models on students' learning collaboratively and critically.

CASE STUDY

Number theory in an upper primary classroom

The participants in the number theory project were two Year 5 and 6 teachers, two teaching assistants (TAs), one university teacher educator and four student teachers who were completing a one-year Postgraduate Certificate in Education (PGCE) ITE course. The focus for the enquiry was stimulating connections between multiples, factors, square numbers and prime numbers by providing learners with representations of integers (Leong et al., 2015) that allow them to make connections and to reason from known facts (Watson et al., 2013). This focus was decided because teachers felt that many of the Year 5 and 6 learners had a procedural understanding of factors and multiples that was restricting their ability to interpret problems and to reason solutions to problems. Learners' descriptions often lacked precision and accuracy. Teachers had also observed that learners were not always equipped with the appropriate language to enable them to explain connections and to reason and discuss problems. However, some of the learners in the classes had a good symbolic understanding of factors and multiples and the properties of composite and prime numbers. Enriching the learning experience for these learners was a feature of the collaborative planning.

All of the participants in the number theory project shared an interest in the learners making reasoned connections between multiples and factors and their relationship with composite, prime and square numbers. All participants were focused on the same goal. However, how each participant reasoned and connected these relationships differed at the start of the project. For example, mathematics teachers could readily agree that 14 is a composite number, or that the first prime number after 14 is 17, but how these known facts are justified and used would depend on how teachers had experienced each relationship in their own mathematics education and teaching experiences. The purpose of the teacher research group model was not to reach consensus from sharing our own preferred teaching approaches, but to make sense of our own experiences and approaches in the context of some of the research that informs learning these concepts so that a research-informed lesson design could be constructed (Swan and Burkhardt, 2014).

REFLECTIVE QUESTION

Think about how you would teach learners to understand and apply the properties of factors, multiples, and composite, square and prime numbers to number theory problems. Reflect on the issues that you have encountered through observation and teaching. How would you explain and justify that 14 is not a prime number but 17 is?

The teacher research group model proposes that research is used to inform the lesson design. The ideas used to stimulate the professional learning within the first stages of the teacher research group were selected by the university teacher educator and were influenced by her own beliefs about how number theory is learnt (Askew, 2015). This is an important feature of the collaborative cycle within the teacher research group because the university teacher educator was presenting research-informed learning models, while the teachers and other participants were representing their own experiences of teaching and learning number theory and knowledge of their teaching contexts and learners. Undoubtedly, tensions between participants will arise when different approaches to learning are shared in contexts such as the teacher research group, and so, as with any community of practitioners, professional dialogue needs to be centred around the shared belief that the purpose of the project was to understand and improve the learning experiences for the learners in the classroom. With this in mind, the group analysed and discussed the proposed learning models in an attempt to design lessons that were informed by expertise about the learners and the context for learning, as well as some of the research that informs how mathematics is learnt.

The university teacher educator highlighted some of the issues associated with a procedural understanding of number theory, and demonstrated how a connected model had the potential to allow learners to reason from their knowledge of multiples to understand factors, and from this knowledge to understand properties of composite, prime and square numbers. The intention was that learners gained a deeper understanding of these aspects of number theory to equip them with the fluency and understanding necessary to apply their knowledge to further number and algebra concepts during their education. This was underpinned by discussion of issues relating to an over-reliance on procedures and definitions in some classrooms, in the absence of reasoned connections (Askew, 2015), alongside knowledge of issues associated with multiplicative reasoning (Watson et al., 2013). The learning models proposed during the collaborative planning were informed by the writing of Askew (2015) and Burton (1994), and were designed by the university teacher educator, having already been used in several classroom projects. The teachers in the teacher research group were able to share approaches that they had used in the past and identified issues relating to the range of prior attainment within the two classes, as well as details of a number of specific learning and development difficulties within the groups.

Using the teachers' knowledge of the prior experiences of the learners, the teacher research group participants were able to design a lesson that could lead to an understanding of factors that builds on the learners existing knowledge of multiples and multiplication facts. This discussion led to the design of a detailed lesson in which they tried to pre-empt possible responses and difficulties. The focus for the participants who were not directly involved in the teaching was to observe and – later – interrogate the responses of the learners to the learning models within the lesson design. All participants were involved in the design and justification of the lesson so that they might be sensitised to noticing the significance of the design in relation to how the learners demonstrate their understanding of the concepts. Although this cycle of the teacher research group involved a single lesson, the professional dialogue was centred on the design of this lesson within a sequence of lessons so that participants' knowledge of connections and key principles within the unit was analysed.

Learners in the two participating classes had previously used the number line to represent multiples and had drawn 'jumps' on the number line. The group discussed how images such as Figure 7.2 had been used to explain why 15 is a multiple of 3 and 5.

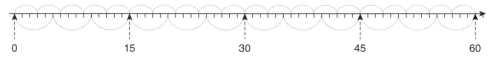

Figure 7.2 'Jumps' on a number line

The teachers felt that most of the learners had a good understanding of multiples and that those who needed support had been encouraged to use counters to group 15 into groups of three or groups of five. The teacher research group discussion centred on the relationship between factors and multiples, as well as how the use of arrays could support understanding and stimulate reasoned dialogue.

Each class teacher introduced the lesson by playing 'guess a rule'. Each learner was asked to say an integer from 0 to 50 and the teacher put the number in the 'rule' or 'not rule' side of the board. To encourage more reasoned dialogue, learners were asked not to call out the rule, but to think about how they might describe the rule. Some learners were asked to predict whether a particular integer would be placed on the 'rule' or 'not rule' side of the board, but were not asked to justify their choice yet. They were asked to talk to the person next to them about the rule, before the class was asked to share descriptions. The learners were able to identify multiples of 3 as the rule, but were not using the terms 'multiple' and 'factor' within their descriptions, preferring 'three times table' or 'add three', as well as some mention of 'can be divided by three'. The teachers explained or prompted the use of the term 'multiple' and then asked the class to explain how they know that 27 is the ninth multiple of 3. Learners were asked why 34 is not a multiple of 3. Observers within the teacher research group noticed more accurate use of the term 'multiple' once it had been modelled by the teacher, as well as the insistence of one of the teachers that the learners rephrase their justifications to use 'multiple' accurately.

The teacher introduced the learners to a table that they were asked to complete so that they could find some more connections. It is designed to use multiples to generate factors to allow learners to understand that 15 is a multiple of 5 because 5 is a factor of 15, as well as identify properties of numbers from their factors. The learners were asked to colour the multiples of 3 in the third row, the multiples of 4 in the fourth row, and so on (see Figure 7.3), so that they could construct the diagram in Figure 7.4.

Figure 7.3   The learner completes the factors table by colouring consecutive multiples

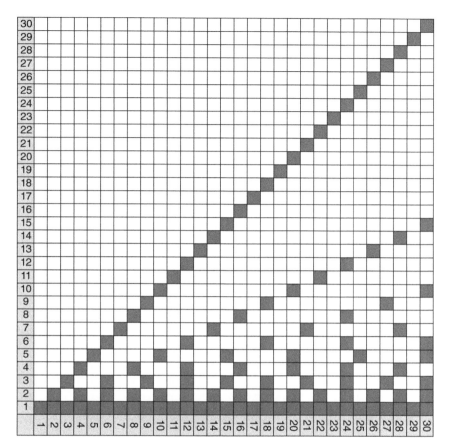

Figure 7.4   Completed factors table

Teachers in both classes led a discussion by asking the learners to start at 15 at the bottom of the table and write down which cells were coloured in. The numbers 1, 3, 5 and 15 were coloured in. They were asked to do this for 12 and 16 too, and then to discuss what they noticed with the person next to them. This stimulated a discussion about factor pairs and, in the case of 16, the 'odd one out' factor. Observers noticed that comments such as 'they are all odd', generated from the factors of 15, were challenged when the learners checked this conjecture with the factors of 12. One pair of learners asked whether they will all be odd for odd numbers. The learners did not use the term 'factor', but set about testing their conjecture using other numbers from the table. Meanwhile, some learners were struggling to make connections between the factor pairs. The teachers brought the class together for a discussion and encouraged the learners to pair the numbers in the list. For example, 24 generated the factors 1, 2, 3, 4, 6, 8, 12 and 24, which were paired from outside in.

Some learners justified the 'odd one out' factor in 16 because 16 is '4 times 4', but were not observed using the term 'square number' at this stage. The teachers asked their classes to find numbers that had exactly four factors. This was no challenge for some of the learners who seemed to have a fluent understanding of factors, even though they were not necessarily using the terms associated with the concept fluently at this stage. These learners were asked to find the number between 31 and 40 that had the most factors. They were asked to justify their answers using area diagrams or arrays. Meanwhile, other learners were asked to use arrays to verify that 24 has eight factors. Learners were encouraged to cut the 6 × 4 array as a starting point if they wanted to, cutting the paper in half to represent 2 × 12 or 3 × 8 arrays, whereas others drew the array patterns in their books.

This support/challenge model of differentiation had been planned in the design of the lesson. The observers in the teacher research group noticed that the learners generally responded well to the choice of representations that they were given to help them justify their answers. They could choose to cut the paper arrays or draw diagrams, which had been planned as a means of supporting the learners' understanding of the structure of the array and its relationship to the four factor pairs, 1 × 24, 2 × 12, 3 × 8 and 4 × 6. They also observed that there were many rich conversations that were taking place which would be impossible to capture in a whole-class discussion. The way that one teacher relinquished control over the pace and direction of the discussions at this stage was noted by the observers. The class discussion that followed differed in each class, but they were both focused on justifying: How do you know that 24 has exactly eight factors? One teacher encouraged her class to justify why 5 is not a factor of 24, with learners offering justifications using the arrays and others using the 'jumps on the number line' representation that they had used in earlier lessons. The second teacher focused the discussion on factors of 24 only.

In the final stage of the lesson, the teacher asked the learners to use the table to find numbers that had exactly two factors. They were asked to justify why 13 had exactly two factors, again using arrays to justify their answers, as diagrams or using counters. The teachers were able to capture the learners' ideas about having one array only, with one row of 13. The lesson ended with the definition of prime numbers having exactly two factors and composite numbers having more than one factor. One class discussed the uniqueness of 1, with only one factor.

During the teacher research group, the participants had planned an enrichment task, available for those who already demonstrated a deeper understanding of the factors and prime numbers. The task was: 'Think about square numbers. How close are they to multiples of four?' This was intended to give learners an opportunity to generalise from specific cases of square numbers presented as arrays. Teachers had decided that they did not need the enrichment task, because they felt that the learners who could confidently list factor pairs at the start of the lesson had still been challenged by the use of the arrays to stimulate reasoning and to justify properties of integers. The teachers noted the challenge inherent to connecting visual and symbolic representations from the array or number line, alongside the impact that this had on some learners' reasoned arguments. This stimulated a discussion about whether enrichment tasks should only be used for those already demonstrating fluency in the concepts learnt, or whether these tasks have the potential to support the understanding of all learners. Perhaps predictably, teachers discussed perceived shortage of time to integrate enrichment tasks into their lessons.

The teacher research group participants identified language as a significant aspect of the lesson. They highlighted details of the conversations and the photographs that they had captured, and were struck by the number of learners who struggled to find appropriate terms to describe what they were noticing. They were able to interrogate these notes and images and discuss the consequences for their planning. For example, the learners maintained the use of the term 'four times table' or informal terms such as 'it's got a 4' when trying to articulate factors of four, or used clumsy terms to try to express divisibility. Participants discussed the significance of using precise and accurate mathematical terms from the beginning of the learners' formal mathematics education. One teacher reflected that these learners had been expected to identify and describe a split-vowel digraph in their phonics education in Year 2 but were not expected to use the term 'multiple of 10' for their 'tens patterns'.

The teacher research group participants perceived the project as valuable and talked positively about its impact on their beliefs about how they should teach these aspects of number theory. One teacher described her perception of the discussions that had taken place in the classroom:

Listening to their explanations today … They had different ways of remembering, different ways of explaining it. I think the whole process has reached all abilities. Everyone has accessed this. If you look at [a pupil with ADHD] this morning … he really was engaged and was able to explain certain aspects of it, which for some of our students, you ask them to explain and they just say, 'Because it is', and he was explaining in more detail because they had put more effort into the practical side and the visual side. We do talk a lot about factors and multiples, but to see it like this is a visual thing that they'll remember … they had to reason … Having that communication with their peers as well … they've been having that dialogue and have been picking up things from the people they've been working with or the people around them as well.

The class teacher was struck by the increase in dialogue in the lesson and the way in which the tasks stimulated dialogue between the learners and between the teacher and learners. One student teacher observed the impact of the tasks on the learners' reasoned discussions:

I haven't taught [number theory] yet but I would use [the lesson tasks]. It's just nice, isn't it … accessible. I think this is so much more visual and much more connecting than looking at stuff on the board or finding numbers. It's deeper, a deeper understanding. This is different and gives much better reasoning behind it.

This suggests that the student teacher had previously imagined (or observed) teaching number theory through definitions and practice, but that the connected model used within the teacher research group had helped him to realise how the structure of the lesson and design of the tasks could allow learners to make reasoned connections, moving away from the more procedural approaches they had used with previous classes.

The lesson review discussion focused on the accessibility of the lesson within a mixed-attainment context. One teaching assistant commented on her perception of the participation and engagement of one learner that she supports:

He was listening and could take on board what he could, even if he did not understand every aspect of it. He really loved working … it gave him the ability to work with his classmates, which is something that he does not always have the opportunity to do.

The class teacher added:

He would have been taken out to be put in a group where we didn't think he would be understanding. Sometimes people just want to dumb it down, when actually the pupils just need a little bit more time. It is all about the questioning.

These comments serve to capture some of the key features of this teacher research group cycle that support the principles behind teaching for mastery. The lesson was designed to allow students to reason from known facts and to make connections between different representations of number, allowing for support and challenge to be planned and implemented as appropriate. The dialogue involved in the professional learning and lesson design situated this lesson within a sequence of lessons that was intended to give learners opportunities to deepen their understanding and to confidently apply their knowledge to problems.

CASE STUDY

Lesson study as a model for teacher enquiry

Now we analyse a second case study, reflecting on how lesson study can be adapted to model good practice in ITE. In particular, we reflect on how lesson study can mediate theory and practice in ITE and how university teacher educators can model pedagogy by conducting lesson study in ITE. There is in fact research evidence that a lesson study experience in ITE can mediate the development of reflective practice (e.g. see Radovic et al., 2014) and provide a transformative experience for student teachers (Baldry and Foster, 2019).

With this tool, student teachers collaboratively develop their practice by constructing their pedagogical understanding as opposed to following rigid lesson structures and plans. The lesson study experience seems to fit with different approaches in the classroom, which emphasise problem-solving, collaboration and an active role for students. We therefore claim that the lesson study experience is a model of good practice for student teachers and more experienced teachers working together.

In this particular case, the teacher educators on the course chose the lessons based on their research experience and their beliefs. This model differs from the Japanese one, where the teachers participating in the lesson study cycle choose a research focus themselves based on the needs of their particular setting and students; in fact, this would not have been possible for inexperienced student teachers working with a 'borrowed 'class. The university teacher educators involved in this study strongly believe in the importance of developing relational understanding (Skemp, 1976) and that mindless repetition could actually be detrimental to learning. They based the choice of lessons on their values about teaching and learning. They chose improving mathematical dialogue as a lesson study focus since they believed that dialogic lessons allow learners to make progress and develop thinking skills. They are opposed to the idea of repetitive teaching and want to trust the ability of all learners to think independently. The current climate in England, with disproportionate importance being placed on high-stakes testing and a culture based on performance often being found in schools (Williams et al., 2014), encourages the use of traditional teaching methods that are not always the most appropriate for learning. Certainly, in some cases, repetitive practice might be necessary for securing memory, but the university teacher educators involved in this case study believe that students develop their understanding the most through experimental and dialogical pedagogy.

REFLECTIVE QUESTION

Different perspectives on teaching and learning are expected in any professional dialogue. How do you think differences should be embraced during collaborative planning?

The university teacher educators involved in this project ensured that the teachers and student teachers did not see the lesson study as a graded activity. In particular, focusing the attention during observations on the learners rather than the teacher, as well as guiding the post-lesson discussion to be mainly concerned about what students did and said, allowed all participants to gain more from the experience, keeping away from performative anxiety. This collaborative, non-threatening climate in fact allowed all participants to experiment with pedagogy and research their own practice without having to deal with external pressures.

Here, a student teacher involved in the lesson study cycle observes how the experience fits within his philosophy of teaching and learning:

> *The main parallel I see between learning to teach and learning maths is that neither is a spectator sport. Students gain very little from watching mathematics being done, as trainees [student teachers] gain limited amounts from just learning about teaching without any practice. And I partly realised this from the lesson studies where the focus was shifted from what the teacher was doing, to analysing what was going on with the learners. And in general I think that it's good to be reminded during your time as a trainee when you are so conscious and aware of yourself that what is going on in the students' heads is far more important than what you are doing.*

> (Archer et al., 2020, p86)

As stated above, the participation of experienced teachers in this project varied due to individual circumstance and constraints (mainly on time). In most cases, there was not enough time available for experienced teachers to plan alongside the student teachers. Baldry and Foster (2019) highlight how the success of lesson study in ITE is subject to establishing a strong working relationship between the school and the ITE provider (in this case, a university); however, lack of time to invest in the experience will result in the more experienced teachers gaining less from the experience.

One teacher involved in the study valued the opportunity to try different approaches:

> *Well, as a teacher I think you get quite set in your ways and I think is nice that you're coming, and say 'try this', and we may try it and it may actually work really well, so I'm quite happy to try it, even though it is a little bit out of my comfort zone – that what I usually do, I think it is quite nice to try it, and if it goes well, keep it for the second lesson, and if it doesn't, I may do what I normally do.*

> (Radovic et al., 2014, p276)

We therefore claim that when the experienced teachers were able to invest time in the planning and post-lesson discussion, the experience was transformative and pedagogical understanding was developed due to the commitment of those involved with the lesson study, their willingness to try something new, and the mutual trust within these groups.

REFLECTIVE QUESTIONS

Think about a lesson study focus you would like to research for one of your classes. Maybe you could think about a 'difficult to teach' topic. How would you go about planning and reflecting on the associate pedagogy? Who will act as a *koshi*?

Discussion of the models of transformative teacher education

The participants' analysis of learners' comments and bookwork suggested that the teacher research group had been successful in making some progress towards meeting the project aims. However, the principles of transformative teacher education discussed at the start of this chapter advocate for a sustained community of teacher enquiry. This teacher research group was formed as part of partnership initiatives between a school and a university; it does not represent an integrated model of research-informed professional learning that can be sustained once the project comes to an end. All participants claimed that they would adopt the lesson design in teaching these aspects of number theory in the future, but we acknowledge that the scope for adopting the teacher research group model as a regular feature of classroom development was limited. Nonetheless, this cycle did serve to demonstrate the potential of the teacher research group model in a primary classroom context – potential to allow participants to share and learn from each other's expertise, and to ensure that the focus of the enquiry is on using this expertise to carefully design lessons and the interrogation of learners' responses to the designed tasks. It is these principles that could provide a basis for local collaborative teacher development, with the scope to contribute to teacher knowledge more generally (Cochran-Smith and Lytle, 2009).

As a model for supporting teaching for mastery, the teacher research group and lesson study structures enable teachers to interrogate learners' responses so that they may respond to learners and adapt how mathematics is presented to the learner. The importance of using evidence to inform the design of the lessons is a critical aspect of collaborative enquiry. This begs the question of where and how teachers will find the stimulus that will inform the design of the lesson. Essentially, teachers must rely on their insight into their learners and their knowledge of the contexts in which they teach, but there must also be a space for teachers to develop their professional knowledge of learning and teaching practices that stimulate connections. In many cases, this means that the stimulus for the collaborative planning does not rest with deciding what will be taught, but interrogates how teachers will teach what is to be taught (Marton et al., 2019). In the example of factors and multiples in the teacher research group discussed in this chapter, teachers were open to ways of developing a connected understanding of number theory that moved away from an over-reliance on definitions and procedures. The teacher research group cycle raised important questions about differentiation, language, dialogue and enrichment through the analysis of only one lesson. These issues already existed for the teachers, but the teacher research group provided the stimulus to address them through lesson design and reignited the participants' enthusiasm for developing their professional knowledge. These encounters are not going to offer a 'quick fix' for the issues that they expose, but do offer a vehicle for transformation over time.

CHAPTER SUMMARY

Key points covered in this chapter are:

- professional learning that is at the heart of teacher research group and lesson study empowers the teacher to translate research into practice, taking ownership of the focus of the enquiry;

- collaborative lesson design and enquiry, including but not limited to teacher research group and lesson study, have the potential to transform classrooms;
- focusing on careful lesson design, justification of pedagogical choices and interrogation of learners' responses has the potential to contribute to a climate that fosters deep conceptual understanding and reasoning;
- authentic transformations require a commitment to sustained collaboration and enquiry within communities of professional learning.

Further reading

Archer, R., Morgan, S. and Swanson, D. (2020) *Understanding Lesson Study for Mathematics: A Practical Guide for Improving Teaching and Learning*. Abingdon: Routledge (in press).

This book, written for teachers, provides an introduction to lesson study as well as details on ten individual primary and secondary mathematics lessons. Each chapter includes a description and analysis of the lesson study cycle, as well as references to the literature that informs the pedagogical choices in the lesson and some general understanding developed from the experience.

References

Archer, R. (2016) 'Lesson study in initial teacher education: students' positioning analysed through the lens of figured worlds'. In G. Adams (ed.), *Proceedings of the British Society for Research into Learning Mathematics*, 36(1): 13–18.

Archer, R., Morgan, S. and Swanson, D. (2020) *Understanding Lesson Study for Mathematics: A Practical Guide for Improving Teaching and Learning*. Abingdon: Routledge (in press).

Askew, M. (2015) *Transforming Primary Mathematics*. Abingdon: Routledge.

Baldry, F. and Foster, C. (2019) 'Lesson study in mathematics initial teacher education in England'. In R. Huang, A. Takahashi and J. Pedro da Ponte (eds), *Theory and Practice of Lesson Study in Mathematics: An International Perspective*. Cham: Springer, pp577–94.

Bamber, S. (2018) 'Translating research into practice through collaborative planning'. In F. Curtis (ed.), *Proceedings of the British Society for Research into Learning Mathematics*, 38(3): 1–6.

Burton, L. (1994) *Children Learning Mathematics: Patterns and Relationships*. Hemel Hempstead: Simon & Schuster Education.

Cochran-Smith, M. and Lytle, S.L. (2009) *Inquiry as Stance: Practitioner Research for the Next Generation*. New York: Teachers College Press.

Cordingley, P. (2015) 'The contribution of research to teachers' professional learning and development'. *Oxford Review of Education*, 41(2): 234–52.

Darling-Hammond, L. (2017) 'Teacher education around the world: what can we learn from international practice?' *European Journal of Teacher Education*, 40(3): 291–309.

Leong, Y.H., Ho, W.K. and Cheng, L.P. (2015) 'Concrete–pictorial–abstract: surveying its origins and charting its future'. *The Mathematics Educator*, 16(1): 1–18.

Marton, F., Cheung, W.M. and Chan, S.W.Y. (2019) 'The object of learning in action research and learning study'. *Educational Action Research*, 27(4): 481–95.

Radovic, D., Archer, R., Leask, D., Morgan, S., Pope, S. and Williams, J. (2014) 'Lesson study as a zone of professional development in secondary mathematics ITE: from reflection to reflection-and-imagination'. *Proceedings of the 8th British Congress of Mathematics Education*, University of Nottingham, 14–17 April, pp271–8.

Skemp, R.R. (1976) 'Relational understanding and instrumental understanding'. *Mathematics Teaching*, 77: 20–6.

Stigler, J.W. and Hiebert, J. (1999) *The Teaching Gap: Best Ideas from the World's Teachers for Improving Education in the Classroom*. New York: Free Press.

Swan, M. (2005) *Improving Learning in Mathematics: DfES Standards Unit*. Available at: http://tlp. excellencegateway.org.uk/pdf/Improving_learning_in_maths.pdf

Swan, M. and Burkhardt, H. (2014) 'Lesson design for formative assessment'. *Educational Designer*, 2(7).

Watson, A., Jones, K. and Pratt, D. (2013) *Key Ideas in Teaching Mathematics: Research-Based Guidance for 9–19*. Oxford: Oxford University Press.

Williams, J., Ryan, J. and Morgan, S. (2014) 'Lesson study in a performative culture'. In O. McNamara, J. Murray and M. Jones (eds), *Workplace Learning in Teacher Education*. Dordrecht: Springer, pp151–67.

Zeichner, K. (2003) 'Teacher research as professional development for P-12 educators in the U.S.'. *Educational Action Research*, 11(2): 301–25.

8

DEVELOPING AND SUSTAINING MASTERY IN EARLY CAREER TEACHERS

HELEN FARMERY AND ANNE MULLIGAN

KEYWORDS: COLLABORATIVE; INITIAL TEACHER EDUCATION (ITE); BEGINNER TEACHER; MASTERY APPROACH; SUSTAINABILITY; ALIGNMENT

CHAPTER OBJECTIVES

Through the lens of the ITE provider, this chapter will:

- explore the challenges faced and strategies used to achieve a beginner teacher/tutor shared belief in an approach to the teaching and learning of mathematics over the course of a three-year undergraduate primary ITE programme;
- consider how those who are leading on mathematics mastery in primary schools are attempting to empower teachers and sustain shared belief in a particular mathematics pedagogy;
- reflect on the alignment of university and school mathematics teacher educators in a pedagogical approach for children;
- consider the application of this approach to other contexts and school phases.

Introduction

To teach for this kind of mastery teachers themselves need a deep structural understanding of mathematics, an awareness of the range and variety of situations in which a mathematical concept or principle can be experienced, and confidence in exploring the connections that are always there to be made in understanding mathematics.

(Haylock, 2016)

Student teachers at the beginning of their initial teacher education (ITE) programme already have a powerful relationship with mathematics based on their own positive and negative school experiences. Their experiences fall into two distinct domains: one categorised by their success or failure in tests ('I am good/rubbish at maths') and the other by their desire to reject or replicate a particular school teacher ('my maths teacher was good/rubbish'). This distinction between mathematics subject knowledge and mathematics pedagogy, and the perceived importance of one over the other, has been grappled with for many years, and with the mastery agenda we seem to be grappling with it more than ever. The more we consider mastery approaches to teaching mathematics, the more blurred the two become, and drawing any distinction between the two – by ourselves as tutors or by beginner teachers – becomes possibly unhelpful (Askew, 2008).

In this chapter, we will be reflecting on how the university mathematics teacher educator (referred to as the tutor) creates an environment in which beginner teachers are confident to rid themselves of past relationships with mathematics and build anew. We will consider how tutors and beginner teachers work within a collaborative culture of change towards a shared understanding of a mastery approach. We will consider how personal belief in the approach can be sustained throughout school-based modules and into teachers' early careers.

What *we* do with our beginner teachers

Beginner teachers will meet many contributors and influencers with varying expertise during their ITE programme, and their conviction in the approaches modelled by their tutors at university can be the key to a sustained mastery approach with learners when they are in school. It is therefore essential that early in the programme, the tutor gains the trust of the beginner teacher.

When beginner teachers and their primary mathematics tutors meet in the first term of their three-year undergraduate programme, time is given to get to know one another. Experiences, interests and anxieties are shared, and tutors attempt to expose any subject-specific fears within a safe learning environment. Early acknowledgement of some shared existence of mathematics anxieties supports the emergence of a trusting community and the beginnings of a learning environment based on social construction.

By listening carefully during this time of new relationship-building, tutors begin to determine the mindset in the group: Who has more distance to go in the pedagogical shift that is being sought, and who may be a possible resistor? Those more resistant to new ideas are more likely to engage in the learning process if tutors acknowledge their existing ideas and use them as tools for unifying ideas (Rusch and Horsford, 2009), but tutors will also seek out early allies. Beginner teachers who show particular openness to new learning or who have positive experience of the desired pedagogy can be key drivers in change and will make potential learning partners for those who need a greater shift in mindset.

Initially perceived confidence in the subject can take some twists and turns. Those who see themselves as weak in mathematics can be open to approaching mathematics differently to previous experience and see their confidence rise. Those who see themselves as strong in the subject can see their confidence waver when a pedagogy that has 'worked' for them exposes weaknesses in deeper understanding. A certain amount of deconstruction or unlearning is often needed, which can be deeply disturbing for some learners, but with careful management these moments can enrich the discourse and be used positively. Many beginner teachers are relieved to find that they are not expected to remember or recall what they used to do, and instead are excited to enter a period of new discovery in their relationship with the subject.

Encouraging reflection on the physical learning environment in which our beginner teachers are expected to learn allows for experiential connections to be made to their emerging pedagogical beliefs. They are encouraged to reflect on their learning accessed in the large lecture theatre compared to that accessed in the classroom; how the light, sound, size and positioning of tables, presence or lack of resources, and wall displays all create differing experiences; how the teacher's presence changes in the two environments; how the students perceive the teacher in the two environments; and how students show differing willingness to question, talk, explore and investigate within the two environments.

Tutors are open and challenging about the learning environment without being authoritative, providing further opportunities for pedagogic discussion: 'I spotted you nodding off' opens up a discussion on the advantages of a dialogic and active classroom, while 'Why didn't you have a go at solving the problem?' opens up discussion on meaningful task design and invested interest. We are looking for an internal shift, and while authoritative teachers may change external behaviours (Sergiovanni, 2007), they may fail to develop long-term commitment to the desired outcome.

From the start of the programme, tutors use videos of themselves teaching children. This strategy of student teachers seeing their tutors in the professional role they aspire to adds validity to these early relationships. The benefit of the tutor being seen less as an expert on a stage separated from what the students are learning to be, and more as a facilitator within a familiar environment, begins to emerge. The students' discourse opens up – their reactions, responses and questions indicate development of a trustful environment and possible emerging shifts in personal beliefs.

Firmly grounded in a socio-constructive approach and adherence to Bruner's (1966) theory of active, iconic and symbolic representation, students' understanding of mastery emerges predominantly through their own solving of appropriately challenging mathematical problems. Problems that require the use of action, imagery and talk to explore mathematical relationships and structures and make generalisations (Wing et al., 2014) are carefully selected, and tutors are explicit in identification of the cognitive connections that the teachers are expected to make when solving the problems set for them. Groups consider their active experience of manipulating the resources and the images that the resources produce. They record and analyse the problem-solving language and look for connections between their actions, images and spoken words. Deep consideration of the connections made to previous experience and knowledge supports beginner teachers' greater depth of conceptual understanding.

REFLECTIVE QUESTION

How do your beginner teachers view you in your role as tutor or school mentor?

- As the anticipator of questions and problems that might come up, and therefore as the finder of answers and solutions that create the tracks for them to follow?
- As the provider of the outcome, the planner of what needs to be done, but they make their own decisions on how to get there?
- As the connector, the person who fits things together in a shared followership?

The following activities are examples of some of the tasks that are used with our developing teachers in workshops.

CASE STUDY

Activity examples

Activity example 1

Here, beginner teachers are asked to use Numicon shapes to prove a conjecture: adding consecutive odd numbers starting from 1 will always create consecutive square numbers (see Figure 8.1). After some trial and lots of manipulation, dialogue and pattern-seeking, images are produced that expose number, shape and spatial ideas that enrich the teachers' mathematical experiences and deepen their conceptual understanding.

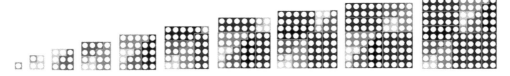

Figure 8.1   Using Numicon shapes to prove a conjecture

Activity example 2

Here, beginner teachers are asked to order 12 separate symbol statements (see Figure 8.2). Some determine quickly that it is a representation of a multiplication table. However, it is their depth of understanding of multiplication facts and structures, as well as how they are represented in familiar numerals, that helps them to decode the symbols. Note how the two-digit products support the determining of which multiplication table is represented and how knowledge of the pattern of the multiples of 1 and multiples of 11 help. Here, tutors emphasise that such activities support mastery of multiplication facts and demonstrate to beginner teachers the need to provide opportunities for learners to deepen number sense and fluency beyond the mere memorisation of multiplication tables.

Unsorted   Sorted

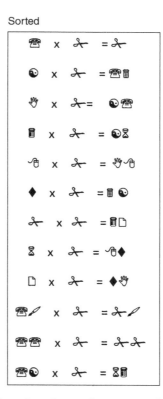

Figure 8.2   Supporting mastery of multiplication

RESEARCH

Developing problem-solving through dialogue

Expected group problem-solving behaviour and metacognitive questions on engagement with tasks support the beginner teachers in their consideration of the pedagogy as well as the mathematics. It is well known that the use of talk and collaborative group work develops learners'

(Continued)

(Continued)

ability to reason when solving problems, which in turn develops their ability to think for themselves (Mercer and Sams, 2006; Rojas-Drummond and Mercer, 2003; Vygotsky, 1978; Wegerif et al., 2004). Through discussions with others in a group, learning is consolidated, leading to improved understanding (Pijls et al., 2007). Gillies and Haynes (2011) recognise the important role the teacher plays in developing effective group problem-solving behaviour and the need for teachers to be trained in using strategic questioning as part of this role. Their research findings on the positive impact on learners' higher-level thinking and learning highlights the need to include this as part of ITE. Table 8.1 shows some of the questions asked of the student teachers to develop group problem-solving behaviour.

Table 8.1 Developing group problem-solving behaviour

Group problem-solving rules	Problem-solving questions
• You are responsible for your own behaviour. • You must be willing to help any group member who asks. • You may only ask the teacher for help if everyone in the group has the same question.	• How did your group get started? • How did the group join the clues? • What caused some difficulty? • What did you find most helpful? • What might you do differently next time? **Further questions** • What made you bother to solve it in the first place? • How would you have felt if you had been stopped halfway through? • How would you have felt if you had been given the answer just before you solved it yourselves?

The shift from viewing mathematics predominantly through the lens of the learner to also viewing it through the lens of the teacher happens when the beginner teachers have spent time in school. Tutors are able to draw upon students' developing expertise and reflections on their own practical experiences through activities that have greater pedagogical emphasis.

CASE STUDY

Further activity examples

Activity example 3

Using the template in Figure 8.3, beginner and more experienced teachers are tasked with observing primary mathematics lessons (both live and on video) and categorising the elements of the lesson into concrete experience, imagery, symbols and language (Haylock and Cockburn, 2017). By considering the balance of these learning opportunities for children, teachers reflect on the depth of understanding achieved, as well as where possible improvements could be made. In an observed lesson where the mathematical talk is predominantly in the teacher's 'delivery' and the children's mathematics is predominantly represented symbolically on worksheets, it is questioned whether learning has been achieved with any depth, as well as how more connections to all four representations could be made. In the context of the beginner teacher, this strategy for lesson observation focuses the observer on the learning that is taking place and less on the meeting of the teachers' standards (DfE, 2011).

Mathematics.	Year Group _____ Date _____
Record your observation by sorting into the boxes the learning that takes place through action, imagery, conversation and symbols. Reflect on the balance of these different representations. Was there a balance? Was one relied on heavily? Were all children offered equal access to all representations?	
Concrete experience	Imagery
Language	Symbols

Figure 8.3   Lesson observation template

Activity example 4

As more time is spent in school and beginner teachers become more accustomed to the formative assessment of their live lessons, tutors and students – when back on campus – have the opportunity to reflect critically on mathematical pedagogy away from the pressures of meeting teachers' standards (DfE, 2011). This takes place through the use of analysis of documents containing written feedback of their formally observed lessons. In a collaborative and contemplative environment, tutors task beginner teachers with highlighting the moments of encouragement towards or achievement of the desired mastery approach.

Over the course of their three school-based modules, student teachers are required to develop their understanding of the role that concrete resources play in the quality of the learning of mathematics. Initial reflective conversations are based around auditing of the resources available to them in their classrooms. However, this quantitative approach (merely listing the tools) soon progresses to a more qualitative consideration of how purposefully and appropriately the resources are used (EEF, 2017). Through observations of experienced teachers, discussions with school mentors and reflection on their own ability to plan and teach using concrete resources, useful reflections enrich the learning conversations back at university. Consideration of resource availability across age ranges, ability ranges, ease of access, level of choice and appropriateness for task all indicate developing adherence to a pedagogical strategy, and – crucially – their reflection on impact on children's learning indicates an internalised commitment.

REFLECTIVE QUESTION

Indication of a change of practice over time. Which statement best fits your current practice?

- No use of a resource (rejection response).
- Available but still not used (symbolic response).
- Some use but not in its intended form (parallel response).
- Good use but only with a few children.
- Good use with all children (accommodation response).

(based on Coburn, 2004)

As well as being useful indicators of beginner teacher shift in mindset, such learning conversations also expose allegiances. Tutors have asked teachers to reassess old assumptions, beliefs, values and theories, and it is extremely difficult to achieve the required change without the help of the whole community. Yet tutors have very little or no influence over the school learning environments in which beginner teachers are placed, and there are occasions where the beginner teachers find themselves either in a highly non-collaborative environment or an environment where interpretation of effective mathematics pedagogy is different to their emerging beliefs. This produces its own set of challenges, illustrated here by emails to her university tutor from a beginner teacher on her final school-based module.

Hello Beverley,

I am writing to share my sadness with someone. I am sorry I chose you.

I have taught maths for the first time on this placement today. I have never felt so insecure while teaching, not even on my first placement. I was teaching subtraction without regrouping but was not permitted to use a number line. I was 'corrected' many times. I said 'calculations' and the teacher wants me to say 'sums', and I had to say 'the bigger number always comes first' without mentioning the order of the numbers. I could go on and on ...

I mentioned that I felt bad for the children who got the LO straightaway; she said they can't go anywhere because mastery is all about working as a group, that I can just give more 'sums' to them.

This is quite worrying. I mean, I am worried. All the staff are lovely; I'm respected, welcomed, I have a good relationship with everyone, but the amount of nonsense – I am just learning, and I feel like what I've learnt so far from you is being challenged.

Will I survive?

Magda

Hello Beverley,

Here I am sharing my experience again. I have been observed today teaching maths.

I got to school this morning, shared the lesson with my class teacher, and her reaction was, 'I don't think you should do that, you still have time to change it. Other classes will be writing in their books, and we should just introduce the topic normally, and the scheme says you should teach the whole class'. I could not believe what I was hearing. I apologised to her for it not being the type of lesson she wanted, but since she had not made any comment on the planning I sent to her, I thought she was OK with it. I taught it but told her that I would do it differently next time.

The lesson was the introduction of addition with regrouping. I introduced the concept to the whole class. I had set up four tables and each group had a set of addition problems to solve using resources. Loads of discussion, very little writing, loads of enthusiasm. The activity was a carousel: table 1 – comparing and ordering numbers; table 2 – simple addition; table 3 – simple subtraction; and table 4 – addition with regrouping, where I stayed to teach it to each group carefully to avoid misconceptions, and to challenge children further if that was the case. Each table apart from the one I was working with was a recap, with some of those 'convince me', 'why', 'show me how' statements. Every set of activities was differentiated; I made sure I had done everything I could possibly do within my knowledge. The children were engaged throughout, and I was really able to work closely on the new concept with each child.

At the end of the day, CT told me it is wrong but did not explain why. She told me I cannot do this tomorrow. I will have to model what is in the textbook, photocopy its activities, stick it in their books and send them off to solve them. I cannot describe my disappointment and sadness.

Can I meet you on Monday, because I just want to know how to succeed in these conditions where you just have to follow what people tell you to do step by step? I am finding it very difficult.

I am sorry for the long email, but I needed to be heard.

Thank you,

Magda

RESEARCH

Experiences of mastery in school

To pursue how many student teachers were experiencing similar misinterpretations of mastery in school to those expressed in the previous example, final-year students were asked to complete a questionnaire on their experiences of mastery while on placement in schools. The questions asked are shown below.

(Continued)

(Continued)

BA Year 3 questionnaire: mastery

1. Define mastery.
2. Where have you gained this understanding (school, literature, university tutors or others)?
3. Was your school talking about mathematics mastery?
4. What did mastery look like in your school?
5. Did it match your perception?

Of the 31 student teachers questioned as to whether mastery in their school matched their perception of the term, 15 felt their perception of mastery gained from the tutors on campus did not match how it was defined in school or presented in practice. Out of the 11 who responded that it did match their perception, only one defined mastery as aligned with the tutors' perceptions. Five responded with 'not applicable' as they had not heard any reference to mastery when in school. Therefore, only one of the 31 student teachers had seen alignment with school and university in their perception of mathematics mastery, and ten had not gained adequate understanding from (or belief in) tutors for tutors to be confident that they had succeeded in gaining a common shared understanding across the whole group.

Student A

What did mastery look like in your school?
'Mastery' was taken from a textbook. The teachers would say 'you've mastered this' and give children a mastery stamp. I felt that the children who had mastered the concept were not always 100% confident in the concept.
Did it match with your perception?
No I don't believe the school used mastery in the best/most effective way. It seemed that HA children were branded as mastery mathematicians.

Student B

What did mastery look like in your school?
We had 'diving deeper' activities which children were given to deepen their knowledge but these were rarely given to middle and lower ability children.
Did it match with your perception?
It did match my perception at the time where I thought that mastery was only linked to higher ability children but since then I have seen from another perspective that all children are able to reach some sort of deeper and secure knowledge.

Figure 8.4 Survey responses

The most frequently cited reason for lack of alignment came in the 17 out of 31 respondents' reference to mastery seen in school as something to be offered only to those deemed to be higher attainers in mathematics (see Figure 8.4). This practice by some experienced teachers and observed by our beginner teachers goes against one of the fundamental principles of a mastery approach to teaching and learning, as discussed in Chapter 1 – that all learners are capable of achieving mastery (Block and Burns, 1976; Bloom, 1973; NCETM, 2016).

Providing video evidence of a strategy or an approach to teaching and learning in action will support the beginner teacher in moving from deliberation to conviction where tutors and literature have failed. Beginner teachers are asked to observe and consider mastery in action with a child with a diagnosed learning difficulty (see Figure 8.5) so that those who are only experiencing

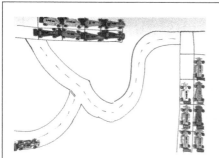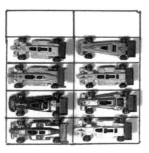

TEACHER: How many cars have you got here, Ari? How many cars have you got in this car park?

ARI: Er, seven?

TEACHER: Seven. Yes! Is that odd or even?

ARI: Odd.

TEACHER: Odd. Well done! But over here, you've got more cars. How many cars have you got here?

ARI: Er, even.

TEACHER: Even, yes, how many cars are there?

ARI: I don't know about that.

TEACHER: Well, you can count them up.

ARI: 1, 2, 3, 4, 5, 6, 7, 8.

TEACHER: Eight, yes. Or you could do 2, 4 (Ari joins in with the count), 6, 8. That's even, you are right.

(Teacher matches the pairs-wise pattern of cars in the drawn car park with a Numicon shape)

TEACHER: We are going to finish off now, Ari. I want you to roll this dice for me, and whatever question it says I am going to ask you. OK? Roll it for me … It says, 'When you were doing odd and even today, did you find anything difficult?'

ARI: Yes. A little bit – if I take one, it is odd (Ari removes a car from the pairs-wise eighth position), and if I put it back it's even. If you add one more to odd, it becomes even.

Figure 8.5 Mastery in action video analysis

mastery in schools as extension questions for higher-attaining children, not for those considered to be weaker in mathematics, can see how all children can be supported to develop mastery. Using footage of one-to-one teacher interventions or small group activities, rather than examples of whole-class teaching, enables beginner teachers to become more disciplined in their noticing (Mason, 2002) and to look beyond what they would see on the surface in a whole-class situation so that they can begin to apply these approaches more effectively in their own practice.

ITE providers support beginner teachers in developing their understanding of what mastery means in terms of teaching and learning mathematics and in being able to apply it in classroom contexts, and we have already mentioned the difficulties experienced by some beginner teachers when this understanding is in conflict with their school experiences. Schools may also experience some difficulties when they adopt a mastery approach to teaching that differs from the approach they have used previously. Schools in this situation must not only consider its immediate implementation as a whole-school pedagogical approach, but also how to ensure sustainability for the future.

The role of a mastery specialist in sustaining the approach in school

To better understand schools' interpretations of mastery approaches to teaching mathematics, a case study was carried out with a partnership school. The school, which we will call Heathrise, is a three-form entry primary teaching school situated in North London. The school has bought into a mathematics scheme based on an East Asian approach to teaching mastery and subscribed to the primary mastery specialist programme run by the National Centre for Excellence in the Teaching of Mathematics (NCETM). We were interested in how the scheme was initially implemented in the school, and met with the mastery specialist (MS) to discuss this.

CASE STUDY

The mastery specialist

Heathrise School had adopted a mastery scheme three years previously and the expectation was that it would be followed to the letter. The initial interest in this scheme stemmed from the need to update the school's current mathematics scheme and the interest of the mathematics subject leader, who had begun to explore the use of a concrete-pictorial-abstract (CPA) approach and the bar model presented at local authority subject leader meetings.

The role of mastery specialist in the school is new and is separate from that of mathematics subject lead. The current mastery lead was in the second year of the two-year programme, and spoke about what it meant to him:

MS Teacher: I have always been passionate about mathematics education and read the NCETM newsletters. The mastery lead role was something the NCETM were offering, which appealed to the school leadership team who were very supportive of me doing it.

The course has confirmed my belief that all children can do mathematics and that the CPA approach is vital for establishing firm foundations in mathematics. I don't observe lessons for mastery, that's the role of the subject leader, but I requested specifically to be a Year 1 class teacher so that I can be closer to where it all starts. I moved from Year 6, so Year 1 has been a challenge, but I am really seeing the benefits of the resources that we use.

Interviewer: How was the scheme implemented?

MS Teacher: It was adopted across the whole school from the start. There was initially two days of training for all staff and the scheme's consultant has been in to develop the ideas. Initially, staff were expected to follow the scheme to the letter, to trust that it will work. Over time, this has been relaxed as the pedagogy is better understood and teachers feel confident to deviate.

The decision to implement it was taken by the senior leadership team without discussion with the wider staff. When asked if this might have been an issue, the MS responded as follows:

MS Teacher: All staff here are accepting of change and embrace opportunities to explore new ideas - the school isn't resistant to change. If there has been any resistance, I don't know about it.

Heathrise School began by adopting a mastery scheme because the senior leaders saw the benefits of this approach to teaching and learning in mathematics. However, they also recognised when aspects of this approach should be adapted to better fit their needs and context. This adapting and developing, which Boylan (2016) discusses, is more conducive to sustaining a mastery approach than simply imposing it on teachers without a shared vision of why it is being implemented. When a leader develops a collaborative learning community where answers are sought through discussion and reflection in an environment of openness, honesty and respect of others' opinions, a change in mindset is likely to be internalised and sustained. Primarily, to lead a programme, the leader must be clear about its desired purpose (Bush and Glover, 2003). The area of difficulty in leadership may arise when the purpose is defined in a more visionary way, sometimes through the use of a vision statement. This is where an element of process enters the common aim, where the key values that underpin the hopes for the mission are shared and possibly challenged (NCSL, 2006).

Successful leadership must be grounded in substance and idea-based (Sergiovanni, 2007), and the leader must be emotionally active and involved (Horner and O'Connor, 2007). This personal belief will mean that articulating the vision to teachers in professional development will not be difficult, but it will need to be supported by a process of implanting the vision so that it can be seen beyond the training room. This is evident in Heathrise School with the role of the mastery specialist. Because he has a clear vision that is shared by the senior leadership team – of how mathematics teaching and learning should be developed – and is committed to this vision, he is better able to support teachers to also share this vision.

When a school newly adopts a programme, it is usual for teachers to be issued with a set of text-books that comes with a package of in-service professional development. How the mastery specialist interprets 'following a mastery programme' may determine to what extent a key message is inter-nalised. If leading on change is reliant on the variable and unpredictable processes of building relationships and communication paths, it is difficult to reconcile it with the prescriptive process of following a programme. Likewise, it is difficult to reconcile that every child is different and that there is no script for teaching children with insistence on adherence to a handbook:

> *[The mastery specialist's] goal is to help your colleagues teach their students effectively not to help them teach programmes better. Programmes or materials are resources for effective instruction. But we teach children not programmes. You will achieve a high degree of success when teachers go beyond recognisably implementing specific practices, to making better decisions within those instructional practices.*

> (Fountas and Pinnell, 2009, p44)

Higgins (2005), in her article on the pedagogy of facilitation, stresses that by adhering to a manual, teachers will not internalise new practices, and that it is the sharing of the concepts and strategies that underlie the materials or manual that will lead to internalised changes. Schwartz (2006) points out that by rigidly following procedures in a rote format, teacher professional expertise is dimin-ished. Teachers taking on a mastery approach are not new to teaching, and their expertise will be of great benefit to the whole learning community. Insistence on adherence to procedures laid out in a textbook could either deskill or produce resistance to the key ideas within. Instead, by using the text-book as a framework from which the teachers build their own ideas and make their own decisions, while acknowledging that all situations are different, the approach becomes contextually responsive (Higgins, 2005). The leader will familiarise themselves with the context in which each teacher works and be able to empathise with the conditions under which they are attempting to achieve the change sought. With this approach, the change is more likely to be internalised. We are reminded of the com-ment by the Heathrise mastery specialist with regard to being able to adapt how the textbooks were used: 'Initially, staff were expected to follow the scheme to the letter, to trust that it will work. Over time, this has been relaxed as the pedagogy is better understood and teachers feel confident to deviate'.

A mastery approach teaches mathematics through connections between concrete representa-tions, images, abstract symbols and talk, and it is important that the underpinning rationale for the approach is understood. Teachers taking on such approaches may at times express a desire to merely be 'shown how to use the purchased materials', but leaders on mastery must be wary of this orientation towards design adherence (Higgins, 2005), and instead encourage a more contextually responsive approach. Teachers need opportunities for thoughtful investigation, reflection and dis-cussion with shared examples in order to deepen the internal shift in commitment to the desired pedagogy and in order to ensure that this commitment is sustained.

Boylan's (2016) discussion on adopting, adapting and developing a mastery approach based on Shanghai mathematics education reflects what Higgins outlines in Table 8.1, and makes it clear that the success of either approach is dependent of the school context and the commitment of those involved. If a school tries to implement a mastery approach on a surface level, then it is likely to be unsuccessful. Sustaining a mastery approach to teaching and learning requires a whole-school approach, supported by the senior leadership team, where time and money are invested to support staff professional development towards a shared conceptual understanding of what mastery involves.

Table 8.2   Comparison of orientations of facilitator's actions towards changing mathematics teaching practice (adapted from Higgins, 2005, p138)

Characteristic of new practice	Orientation of facilitator's actions: facilitation disposed towards design adherence	Orientation of facilitator's actions: facilitation disposed towards contextual responsiveness
Teachers' manual or handbook	Emphasis is given to adhering to the programme design and the handbook.	Emphasis is given to using structural elements to interpret the handbook.
Materials (activities)	Emphasis is given to engaging learners actively with the materials.	Emphasis is given to teachers' understanding of the mathematical purposes and concepts underlying the materials.
Teaching method	Emphasis is given to the experiential effect of activities.	Emphasis is given to learners' representations of their mathematical understandings.
Modelling new practice	Emphasis is given to learners' 'proper' use of the materials.	Emphasis is given to extending concepts in response to students' actions and explanations.

Having an expert as a leader does not promote generative learning (Fountas and Pinnell, 2009); therefore, the lead for mastery must be a learner within the community of enquiry in order that the teachers generate their own personal understanding. The mastery specialist has placed himself as part of the learning community by requesting to teach in Year 1 'to be closer to where it all starts'. This way, he is positioning himself as a developing professional, not an expert. It allows him to remain emotionally active and involved and in a better position to model reflective behaviour, whereas when labelled as an expert, other teachers are more likely to look to him for answers. He is de-emphasising any top-down hierarchy and empowering staff to make their own decisions. He is connecting them to outcomes rather than the means of getting there, giving them space to develop their own thinking and build on their own experiences over time, with careful guidance from more knowledgeable others. The mastery specialist at Heathrise is hopeful that his leadership approach will allow for teachers' internalised belief in practice rather than extrinsic performance of procedures, resulting in greater sustainability of the new pedagogical approach.

CHAPTER SUMMARY

Key points covered in this chapter are:

- engaging in mathematics activities collaboratively is an effective strategy to develop beginner teachers' understanding of mastery in mathematics, and provides the mind shift needed for these beliefs to be sustained;
- beginner teachers can experience a disjuncture between their theoretical understanding of a mastery approach and their experiences of the approach when on school placement;

(Continued)

(Continued)

- schools in which mastery approaches are being implemented successfully are those that are investing in a whole-school approach supported by senior leaders and involving all staff;
- an emphasis on adapting aspects that work well and developing them to suit the context of the school is effective in implementing mastery approaches, rather than strictly adhering to a particular mastery scheme;
- having someone with an interest in and an understanding of the practices and principles of teaching for mastery, who can oversee its development across the school, increases the sustainability of the approach.

Further reading

Griffiths, R., Back, J. and Gifford, S. (2016) *Making Numbers: Using Manipulatives to Teach Arithmetic.* Oxford: Oxford University Press.

Newell, R. (2017) *Big Ideas in Primary Mathematics.* London: SAGE.

These books provide further activity examples to support beginner teachers in their confidence to teach mathematics with a focus on conceptual understanding rather than memory.

Higgins, J. (2005) 'Pedagogy of facilitation: how do we best help teachers of mathematics with new practices?' In H. Chick and J. Vincent (eds), *Proceedings of the 29th Conference of the International Group for the Psychology of Mathematics Education*, 3: 137–44. Melbourne: PME.

This article is referred to in the text and should be read more fully to support teachers in fully understanding the subtleties of contextual responsivity over design adherence when being introduced to new schemes of work.

References

Askew, M. (2008) 'Mathematical discipline knowledge requirements for prospective primary teachers and the structure and teaching approaches of programs designed to develop that knowledge'. In P. Sullivan and T. Wood (eds), *The International Handbook of Mathematics Teacher Education Vol. 1.* Rotterdam: Sense, pp13–35.

Block, J. and Burns, R. (1976) 'Mastery learning'. *Review of Research in Education*, 4(1): 3–49.

Bloom, B.S. (1973) 'Recent developments in mastery learning'. *Educational Psychologist*, 10(2): 53–7.

Boylan, M. (2016) 'Developing frameworks for evaluating and researching the Shanghai Mathematics Teacher Exchange: practices or assemblage'. In G. Adams (ed.), *Proceedings of the British Society for Research into Learning Mathematics*, 36(2): 13–18.

Bruner, J.S. (1966) *Toward a Theory of Instruction Vol. 59.* Cambridge, MA: Harvard University Press.

Bush, T. and Glover, D. (2003) *School Leadership: Concepts and Evidence.* Nottingham: NCSL.

Coburn, E. (2004) 'Beyond decoupling: rethinking the relationship between the institutional environment and the classroom'. *Sociology of Education*, 77(3): 211–44.

Department for Education (DfE) (2011) *Teachers' Standards*. London: DfE.

Education Endowment Foundation (EEF) (2017) *Improving Mathematics in Key Stages Two and Three*. London: EEF.

Fountas, I. and Pinnell, G. (2009) 'Keys to effective coaching: cultivating self-extending teachers in a professional learning community'. *Journal of Reading Recovery*, 8(2): 39–47.

Gillies, R. and Haynes, M. (2011) 'Increasing explanatory behaviour, problem-solving, and reasoning within classes using cooperative group work'. *Instructional Science*, 39(3): 349–66.

Haylock, D. (2016) *Mastery and Understanding Mathematics*. Available at: http://derek-haylock.blogspot. com/2016/02/mastery-and-understanding-mathematics.html

Haylock, D. and Cockburn, A. (2017) *Understanding Mathematics for Young Children: A Guide for Teachers of Children 3–7*. London: SAGE.

Higgins, J. (2005) 'Pedagogy of facilitation: how do we best help teachers of mathematics with new practices?' In H. Chick and J. Vincent (eds), *Proceedings of the 29th Conference of the International Group for the Psychology of Mathematics Education*, 3: 137–44. Melbourne: PME.

Iorner, S. and O'Connor, E. (2007) 'Helping beginning and struggling readers to develop self-regulated strategies: a reading recovery example'. *Reading & Writing Quarterly*, 23(1): 1–17.

Mason, J. (2002) *Researching Your Own Practice: The Discipline of Noticing*. London: Routledge.

Mercer, N. and Sams, C. (2006) 'Teaching children how to use language to solve maths problems'. *Language and Education*, 20(5): 507–28.

National Centre for Excellence in the Teaching of Mathematics (NCETM) (2016) *Teaching for Mastery*. Available at: www.ncetm.org.uk/resources/46830

National College for School Leadership (NCSL) (2006) *Securing Commitment of Others to the Vision: PQH 1.2*. Nottingham: NCSL.

Nijls, M., Dekker, R. and van Hout-Wolters, B. (2007) 'Reconstruction of a collaborative mathematical learning process'. *Educational Studies in Mathematics*, 65: 309–29.

Rojas-Drummond, S. and Mercer, N. (2003) 'Scaffolding the development of effective collaboration and learning'. *International Journal of Educational Research*, 39: 99–111.

Rusch, A. and Horsford, S. (2009) 'Changing hearts and minds: the quest for open talk about race in educational leadership'. *International Journal of Educational Management*, 23(4): 302–13.

Schwartz, R. (2006) 'Supporting teacher learning: reading recovery as a community of practice'. *Journal of Reading Recovery*, 6(1): 49–55.

Sergiovanni, T. (2007) *Rethinking Leadership: A Collection of Articles*. Thousand Oaks, CA: Corwin Press.

Vygotsky, L.S. (1978) 'Mind in society'. In M. Cole, V. John-Steiner, S. Scribner and E. Souberman (eds), *Mind in Society*. London: Harvard University Press.

Wegerif, R., Littleton, K., Dawes, L., Mercer, N. and Rowe, D. (2004) 'Widening access to educational opportunities through teaching children how to reason together'. *Westminster Studies in Education*, 7(2): 143–56.

Wing, T., Tacon, R. and Atkinson, R. (2014) *Number Pattern and Calculating: Numicon Implementation Guide 1*. Oxford: Oxford University Press.

ENDNOTE: THE ASSOCIATION OF MATHEMATICS EDUCATION TEACHERS

www.ametonline.org.uk

The Association of Mathematics Education Teachers (AMET) is an independent voice for mathematics teacher educators in the United Kingdom with membership predominantly from the initial teacher education (ITE) community. The association was established in its current form in 1991 with Derek Haylock as chair and editor of the association's journal, *Mathematics Education Review*.

For almost 30 years, the association has been providing a forum for cutting-edge thinking, ideas and practice to be shared and refined by those working with new and experienced teachers in both primary and secondary phases. AMET's annual conferences bring a like-minded community together to celebrate, inform and develop mathematics teacher education. The association is particularly keen to support teachers and tutors who are new to working with beginner and early career teachers in their teaching of mathematics.

AMET is a participating body of the Joint Mathematical Council of the United Kingdom, an organisation that makes representation and responds to enquiries from government and other policymakers on the advancement of the teaching and learning of mathematics. The council is an important forum for our ITE mathematics tutor voice to be heard.

This book has been developed by AMET committee members who are keen to capture the community's current thinking on mastery and establish that it is a pedagogy grounded in theory and action research which has been espoused by those in mathematics teacher education for many years.

If you are interested in attending our conferences or becoming a member of the association for a small subscription fee, please visit **www.ametonline.org.uk** and complete our online membership form.

INDEX

Note: References in *italics* are to figures, those in **bold** to tables.